The Survival Agenda
of the
Greatest Generation:

Lost in the Crush of the Information Age

Joseph A. Bagnall

The Survival Agenda
of the
Greatest Generation:
Lost in the Crush of the Information Age

———————————

ISBN: 978-1514123409
1514123401

Create Space Independent Publishing Platform

Printed in the United States of America

To the American Federal Union:

Past, Present, and Future

Acknowledgements

A special thank-you to my wife, Naomi Bagnall, for assistance in preparing the manuscript. I also appreciate the work on the cover by my daughter, Ashley Jo Davis.

Cover Photographs

Clockwise from top left:

Franklin D. Roosevelt
Albert Einstein
Edward Teller
Harry S. Truman
Dwight D. Eisenhower
Walter Cronkite
J. Robert Oppenheimer
Jimmy Carter
Ronald Reagan
Eleanor Roosevelt
Wendell Willkie
Norman Cousins
George H. W. Bush
Earl Warren

Center:

John F. Kennedy

Photo Credits

Albert Einstein Library of Congress, Prints and Photographs Division, Digital ID eph. 3b46036

Edward Teller. Lawrence Livermore National Laboratory photo.

President Harry S. Truman. US Army film, courtesy of the Harry S. Truman Library.

President Dwight D. Eisenhower. Courtesy of the Dwight D. Eisenhower Library.

Norman Cousins. PD-USGOV-NASA.

Chief Justice Earl Warren. Harris and Ewing Photography, in the public domain.

President George H. W. Bush, White House photo, Library of Congress Prints and Photographs Division.

President Ronald Reagan. Official White House photograph, courtesy of the Library of Congress Prints and Photographs Division, LC-USZ62-13040.

President John F. Kennedy. White House photo, courtesy of the Kennedy Presidential Library and Museum, Boston.

Eleanor Roosevelt. Franklin D. Roosevelt Presidential Library and Museum.

J. Robert Oppenheimer, Director of the Manhattan Project, 1944. U S Department of Energy photograph, in the public domain.

Wendell Willkie. Presidential campaign poster of 1940, in the public domain

President Jimmy Carter. Official White House photograph, Library of Congress 3IjA770324.

President Franklin D. Roosevelt. Franklin D. Roosevelt Presidential Library and Museum.

Walter Cronkite. Steve Friedman, copyright CBS Inc., all rights reserved, (#86005). Used with permission.

Back Cover Photograph

Joseph A. Bagnall. Melinda Finn.

Contents

Appendix

"Disarmament," address delivered in Washington, DC, December 11, 1959.

New Twelve-Point Agenda in Foreign Policy," address delivered in Washington, DC, June 14, 1960.

Prologue

"The dogmas of the quiet past are inadequate for the stormy present. The occasion is piled high with difficulty and we must rise with the occasion. As our case is new, so we must think anew and act anew. We must disenthrall ourselves."

—Abraham Lincoln

"Now the trumpet summons us again—not as a call to bear arms, though arms we need—but a call to bear the burden of a long twilight struggle, year in and year out, rejoicing in hope, patient in tribulation—a struggle against the common enemies of man: tyranny, poverty, disease and war itself. Can we forge against these enemies a grand and global alliance, North and South, East and West, that can assure a more fruitful life for all mankind? Will you join in that historic effort?"

—John F. Kennedy

"The only limit to our realization of tomorrow will be our doubts of today. Let us move forward with strong and active faith."

—Franklin D. Roosevelt

Introduction

Tom Brokaw, former news anchor at NBC, has written about the generation that saved democracy and capitalism in the Great Depression and played a major role in winning World War II. I share his opinion that it was our greatest generation.

The greatest generation also created the United Nations, which is composed of legislative, executive, and judicial branches. Not only does it resemble the basic structure of the US government, but it also has at its disposal, the Universal Declaration of Human Rights (UDHR), which is highly reflective of the substance of the American Bill of Rights.

As Ambassador to the United Nations during the Truman administration, Eleanor Roosevelt chaired the committee that drafted the Universal Declaration of Human Rights. Her outstanding leadership led to the General Assembly ratification of the Universal Declaration with the smashing vote of forty-eight to zero. But it still was not unanimous; seven nations, led by the Soviet Union, abstained.

Heroes of the greatest generation have boldly called for the strengthening of the United Nations and the development of world law. They are chronicled in this volume and hereby presented to a generation that either has ignored them or has never been aware of their message.

The three branches of the United Nations could be strengthened and developed into a system of checks and balances, thereby averting tyranny at the highest international level. The Universal Declaration of Human Rights could also be codified into enforceable world law. Do we have the faith, the courage, and the will to make it happen?

President Kennedy was a strong advocate of world peace through the development of world law, and he also proposed a worldwide program of conservation. But few citizens are aware of this because the media have concentrated—and capitalized—on his wit, style, and charm; focused on sentimentality; and emphasized the sensational facets of his life—and death.

President Kennedy receives scant attention on the anniversary of his birth, because we "celebrate" his life and times on the anniversary of his death. This may be commercially advantageous, but it distorts his image and obscures his legacy.

As we move toward the JFK centenary on May 29, 2017, it is preeminently the time for Kennedy to be defined as something more than the central figure in a murder mystery or the princely figure of Camelot. In addition, a book about his legacy and its meaning for our time, is far more relevant than a book about his private life. And a book that promotes the anniversary of Kennedy's birth should be at least as important as one that promotes the anniversary of his death.

I have been privileged to honor JFK on the seventieth, seventy-fifth, and one-hundredth anniversaries of his birth.

For the seventieth anniversary of his birth, I wrote and produced a TV documentary entitled *John F. Kennedy's Lost Pathway to Peace*, which aired nationally on TBS and regionally on KCET, Los Angeles, on May 29, 1987.

For the seventy-fifth anniversary I edited the first edition of *President John Fitzgerald Kennedy's Grand and Global Alliance;* I was interviewed about the book by Charles Osgood on May 29, 1992, on the CBS Radio network.

For the one-hundredth anniversary I have published *The Survival Agenda of the Greatest Generation,* a book in which President Kennedy emerges as an authoritative spokesperson for environmental and thermonuclear issues, not only for his time but also for the twenty-first century.

Endnotes document the rare, controversial statements found in chapter 3 entitled "Peace Seekers from the Greatest Generation." Seventeen lengthy documents, located in the appendix, serve as source material for the Kennedy quotations in chapter 4 entitled "Uncovering the Kennedy Legacy." These documents not only provide immediately accessible documentation, but also give the reader a rare opportunity to study JFK's quotations in context.

It is my strong conviction that the Universal Declaration of Human Rights should be widely disseminated. This great document may be studied in its entirety in the appendix.

Joseph A. Bagnall
Oceanside, California
July, 2015

CHAPTER ONE

The Survival Hot List:
Conquering the Seven Deadly Trends

Without the benefit of a survey or a poll, it nonetheless seems certain that most Americans think of human survival in terms of economic gain and material comfort. Few people have the time to devote to thermonuclear or environmental issues. Most of those who read books concentrate on fictional escapism, celebrities, sports, and strategies for success. Even the few books about important international issues have minor significance in the larger context of human survival.

In addition, a significant portion of broadcast and print journalists routinely demonize environmental causes and peace efforts. But with all these impediments and others, survival in the twenty-first century is still within the realm of human possibilities. The window of opportunity is swiftly closing, however, and will soon be shuttered.

Seven Deadly Trends

Seven deadly trends are rapidly advancing in the 21st Century. The first trend is *nuclear proliferation,* which is as current as today's headlines. While some nations are trying to tell others who can be in the nuclear club, the nuclear club is expanding, and the possibility of thermonuclear obliteration is growing.

The second trend is *international terrorism,* which has become a constant threat to every nation and could be effectively stifled with a mighty collective response from all nations.

The third trend is *global warming,* which will alter earth's shorelines and diminish the land mass worldwide; it has already contributed to some nasty weather patterns in the earth's choice regions for human habitation.

The fourth trend is *destruction of the rainforests,* with the resultant loss of potential medicinal finds and the increased alteration of weather patterns.

The fifth trend is *the depletion of the ozone layer.* According to NASA, the ozone hole has grown larger than the North American continent, opening a vast area to a bombardment of UV-B, which weakens human and animal immune systems and impairs photosynthesis and plant metabolism. This form of radiation will penetrate the oceans and cause a slower growth rate for plankton, thereby reducing the available food supply for other forms of sea life.

The sixth trend is *acid rain,* which is destroying forests and lakes in eastern Canada, the northeastern United States, Germany, and eastern Europe. In some regions the dumping of calcium carbonate into dead lakes is underway in an attempt to revive them.

The seventh deadly trend is *apathy.* Scientists have described the deadly trends, and national leaders are tinkering with them, in an effort to involve people in their resolution. But the people seem to know that nothing can be done short of an intensive worldwide effort.

As a matter of fact, none of the seven deadly trends will be resolved without enforceable worldwide control. The odds, however, are heavily stacked against a significant international effort to save the battered environment. The odds are even more heavily stacked against an international effort to control nuclear weapons. But the odds, unfortunately, are not heavily stacked against the destruction of human civilization in the 21st Century.

Many options are before us. We can ignore or misrepresent the world we live in—and drift toward a grim, unintended fate. We can engage in crisis-to-crisis improvisation with little chance for meaningful success. Or we can engage in a long-term international effort to control nuclear weapons and curb environmental threats. For those who feel that long-term international planning cannot be achieved, it might be instructive to consider "The Theoretical Basis for Hope" and the vital words of the "Peace Seekers from the Greatest Generation."

CHAPTER TWO

The Theoretical Basis for Hope:
Evolution of the Social Contract

In the twenty-first century, all life is tentative on an environmentally battered and politically challenged planet. Thermonuclear and environmental issues go unresolved because there is no prospect for solution without a vigorous international effort, and there is no hint of a cooperative approach in sight. The hope for human survival, however, has a foundation in the philosophical underpinning of the American nation.

The theoretical foundation for the American Declaration of Independence and the United States Constitution lies in social-contract theory. It was from the writings of John Locke, Thomas Hobbes, and Jean-Jacques Rousseau that our founding fathers drew their rationale for the institutionalization of freedom and the practice of the consent of the governed.

Thomas Hobbes identified freedom as a natural condition for humankind, but he also explained that in their natural state humans experienced "nasty," "brutish," and "short" lifespans. Our primitive ancestors, it seems, were free to rape, decapitate, cannibalize, and rely on a few savage kinsmen to assist in the struggle to survive.

A social contract emerged in this chaos. A clan of individuals tacitly agreed to surrender negative freedoms to commit savagery against one another. They set rules of conduct within their society. They began to institutionalize and protect positive freedoms, and they based decision-making on the consent of the governed. The clan, therefore, became the first political unit in the survival process, and the first institution to incorporate rudimentary ethical facets of modern civilization.

Clans evolved into tribes, where cooperation and bonding were strengthened through rules and laws, primitive religious rituals, symbols, and perhaps a flag. In this evolutionary process, humankind institutionalized freedom, developed a rule of law, and resolved to base decision-making on the consent of the governed.

As nomadic tribes became sedentary, rules for the village evolved into more sophisticated social contracts, which eventually culminated in city-states and thenceforth into modern nation-states.

In this long process, the evolutionary social contract became not only the catalyst in the development of civilization, but also, in every progression, *a survival device.*

The politics of survival were operative at the Philadelphia Convention in 1787. American patriots fashioned the ultimate social contract, a political masterpiece, and the most enduring written constitution on earth.

But why was the new constitution necessary? Born in the chaos of a ramshackle government under the Articles of Confederation, the federal constitution was an agreement between diverse factions to bring political order and economic stability to a fragmented, powerless new nation.

Under the failed Articles of Confederation, large states, small states, free states, and slave states were loosely combined. They were thirteen in number; economically, politically, and culturally diverse; and fragmented to the point where the prospect of an enduring nation—a "United" States—seemed dim.

Foreign nations cast suspicious eyes upon our failure to create an effective national executive. When a congressional committee attempted to conduct diplomacy, British diplomats asked if we were seeking one treaty or thirteen. The currency was not uniform, which created economic confusion at home and abroad; disputes between states over navigation of waterways and questions of commerce sometimes led to armed clashes; and, finally, Congress could not levy and collect taxes or build an adequate national defense.

Problems under the Articles of Confederation could not be characterized as nasty, brutish, or savage, but their resolution was crucial for the survival of the new nation and essential for the preservation and maintenance of freedom.

In this crisis American patriots sought commonality in "a more perfect union." They needed a new structure that was politically viable and economically solvent. The American federal system that emerged from the Philadelphia Convention of 1787 propelled the evolutionary social contract to new heights. The new federal republic featured a national capstone composed of legislative, executive, and judicial branches with separate and limited powers. This approach prevented central tyranny, through a dynamic interplay of "checks and balances" and a division of power between the national government and the states.

The American federal union has harbored ideological differences, fostered an environment of pluralism and diversity, and underwritten personal freedoms through an appended Bill of Rights, It established a uniform system of justice through an effective system of federal courts, capped off with a Supreme Court. And it fulfilled the long-term goals of its makers by providing for the common defense, promoting the general welfare, and guaranteeing liberty for its founders and for their posterity.

The American Constitution has survived the transition from an agricultural nation to a technologically advanced industrial nation. It has survived the crises of civil war, two world wars, and major economic upheavals. It has designated and preserved national forests and national parks. The oldest written constitution on earth, it has been amended a mere twenty-seven times. It is the ultimate social contract, and if humankind seeks resolution of the deficiencies of the United Nations and control over nasty environmental hazards and brutal thermonuclear threats, it can be a model for world governance.

CHAPTER THREE

Peace Seekers from the Greatest Generation

Our eyes are focused on the screens of our smart phones, tablets, and laptops. We stand in long lines to purchase the latest electronic gadget. We focus our thoughts to fit the specified parameters of the tweet. We substitute social media for socialization. And we all wade ankle deep in the shallow tides of the information age.

Our business goals rarely extend beyond maximizing profit for the upcoming quarterly report. Our political goals are largely designed to guarantee a win in the next election.

Gone is the period when cities had as many as five competing daily newspapers. Gone also is the time when sophisticated magazines were proudly displayed on coffee tables and informative discussions and debates were evoked by their content.

The era of print journalism has been obliterated by the electronic sound bite delivered by the Internet and television. New media have furnished so many outlets for information and entertainment that society has become fragmented, if not thoroughly confused.

The time has passed when the masses made a living wage and one salary met the mortgage, the car payment, and family expenses. Our modern economy requires two working parents and a preschool for most children. In this environment, it seems, the masses are preoccupied, on a full-time basis, with making a living. That vital goal seems to summarize our concern with survival issues.

Does our modern environment preclude the possibility of collective action to achieve long-term survival goals? Is it possible to unify and rally in support of human-survival issues? Is the survival perspective that was shared by leaders of the greatest generation worthy of our consideration today? Or should we follow the lead of well-financed right-wing spokespersons who dub peace movements and environmental causes the work of conspirators and subversives?

Is anyone concerned about the abandonment of a survival agenda in the face of twenty-first-century environmental deterioration and colossal thermonuclear threats? Is there anyone who will pause, in the exhilaration of the information age, to consider the advice of some of the important voices of the past? Here are a few of those voices.

Albert Einstein

Albert Einstein had deep insight into the horror of atomic weaponry. His book, *Einstein on Peace*, is a testament to his dedication to the attainment of world law.

In a broadcast on NBC television on February 19, 1950, he stated that "a supra-national judicial and executive body [should be] set up and empowered to decide questions of immediate concern to the security of the nations." Even this "restricted world government," Einstein said, "would considerably reduce the imminent danger of war."[1]

J. Robert Oppenheimer, director of the Manhattan Project, has often been called the "Father of the Atomic Bomb." After the bomb was successfully tested and dropped on Japan, Dr. Oppenheimer was horrified and deeply guilt-ridden. His conscience compelled him to oppose the development of the more powerful hydrogen bomb. As a result, his patriotism was questioned, his security clearance was stripped by the Atomic Energy Commission, and he suffered with others who had been branded as subversive in the McCarthy era.

For the balance of his life, Dr. Oppenheimer insisted that if the human race was to survive, nuclear weapons must be internationally controlled.

President Lyndon B. Johnson reinstated Dr. Oppenheimer in 1963 and, in a public ceremony, gave him the Enrico Fermi Award. Broken and frail, Dr. Oppenheimer died of throat cancer four years later.

Edward Teller, father of the H-bomb, knew that his hydrogen bomb had made the atomic bomb obsolete. Beginning in the mid-1950s, atomic weapons performed a new minor function. They became merely the trigger on Teller's hydrogen bomb.

Before Teller, the power of atomic weapons had been measured in the kiloton range: one kiloton was the equivalent of one thousand tons of TNT. The power of hydrogen bombs is now measured in the megaton range: one megaton equals one million tons of TNT.

If exploded over a modern city, one mid-sized hydrogen bomb would blast a crater five miles in

Edward Teller

circumference and 440 feet deep. It would spread firestorms fifty miles in all directions. The center of the explosion would be near the temperature of the sun, and the atomic trigger would scatter toxic radioactivity far and wide. All of this horror could be released by just one mid-range hydrogen bomb, deliverable by one missile.

In his book *The Legacy of Hiroshima*, Dr. Teller wrote "Our goal in the final analysis cannot be merely to do away with arms and armies. We must instead work for elimination of irresponsible and illegal acts of independent nations. We must work for the establishment of a world authority sustained by moral force and physical force—a worldwide government capable of enforcing worldwide law and worldwide disarmament."[2]

This bold assertion seems to contradict much of what Dr. Teller had to say, over the years, in terms of treaties and international diplomacy.

President Franklin D. Roosevelt, in discussions with Winston Churchill, even before US entry into World War II, insisted that the institution he later named the United Nations must be built. In the early stages of the war, Roosevelt's war aims were embodied in his famous Four Freedoms speech. In this address he said that we sought freedom of speech—everywhere in the world, freedom of religion—everywhere in the world, freedom from want—everywhere in the world, and freedom from fear—"which," FDR said, "translated into world terms, means a world-wide reduction of armaments to such a point and in such a thorough fashion that no nation will be in a position to commit an act of physical aggression against any neighbor—anywhere in the world."

It is therefore abundantly clear that FDR strongly supported the United Nations and the cause of world disarmament. During the war, due to the strict secrecy of the Manhattan Project, he was almost exclusively aware of the horror of the coming atomic age.

President Truman

President Harry S. Truman began his administration in a courageous way. In his January 21, 1946, State of the Union address, Truman called for development of the United Nations until we recognize the world as one society.[3]

His dedication to the newly formed United Nations was steadfast. He worked through the United Nations to implement virtually all of his foreign policy goals.

In response to a Communist North Korean invasion of South Korea, Truman organized a United Nations "police action" to contain North Korea at the thirty-eighth parallel. Twenty-two nations resisted the aggression under a UN flag and the flags of their respective countries. United States forces were only partially mobilized with the limited objective of protecting the South Korean government.

South Korea was successfully defended, and under the next president, Dwight David Eisenhower, a treaty was signed, recognizing the thirty-eighth parallel as the boundary between the two Koreas.

Former first lady **Eleanor Roosevelt** was appointed US Ambassador to the United Nations by President Truman.

As the dynamic chairperson of the commission that drafted the Universal Declaration of Human Rights, she was able to help formulate and guide this epic document past the Soviet bloc, and other US adversaries, and get it ratified by the General Assembly of the United Nations. The vote was forty-eight to zero. But it was not really unanimous, because seven nations, led by the Soviet Union, abstained.

For Mrs. Roosevelt's distinguished work, President Truman, and many others, referred to her as "First Lady of the World."

She was the key person in propelling the freedoms contained in the American Bill of Rights to the international level.

If James Madison can be called the "Father of the Bill of Rights," then Eleanor Roosevelt must be recognized as the person who reframed those rights and elevated them to the world stage.

Eleanor Roosevelt at the UN

Since its ratification on December 10, 1948, the Universal Declaration of Human Rights has become the most translated document in the world. Most new national constitutions, national laws, and recent treaties have been influenced by it. The tenth of December has been designated by the UN General Assembly as Human Rights Day, but the United States has failed to celebrate it—or to commemorate the fiftieth anniversary of the ratification of the UDHR.

Every president since 1945—President Carter in particular—has reminded other nations of failures to implement human rights. The hope for the survival of humankind in a world of peace, justice, and freedom hinges on the swift codification of the tenets of the UDHR into enforceable world law.

Heroic national leaders have left us an American foundation for world order with three branches of international government and a Universal Declaration of Human Rights. It is left for us to accomplish the lesser part.

President Eisenhower

President Dwight David Eisenhower was the Supreme Allied Commander in the European theater of World War II. He commanded Allied forces on June 6, 1944, in Operation Overlord, the largest invasion force in the history of humankind.

Eisenhower was a distinguished five-star general who chronicled his war record in his multi-volume opus entitled *Crusade in Europe.*

As president, Eisenhower ended the war in Korea and served for two terms without involving the United States in military action anywhere in the world. His presidential memoirs were appropriately titled *Waging Peace.*

In his address at the United Nations on September 22, 1960, President Eisenhower said, "Thus we see as our goal, not a super-state above nations, but a world community, embracing them all, rooted in law and justice."[4]

On other occasions Eisenhower also referred to the need for a world community under law. In his State of the Union address in 1959, he lamented, "All peoples are sorely tired of the fear, destruction, and waste of war. As never before, the world knows the human and material costs of war and seeks to replace force with a genuine rule of law for all nations."[5] In his State of the Union address in 1960, he also called for the empowerment of the International Court of Justice and the development of world law.

Chief Justice Earl Warren

Other prominent voices joined the chorus: Immediately after the Hiroshima bombing, Norman Cousins, editor of *Saturday Review*, wrote the first of hundreds of weekly editorials, gave numerous addresses, and wrote important books—all advocating that the United States pursue world peace through the development of world law. Louis B. Sohn and Grenville Clark collaborated on an important Harvard University Press book titled *World Peace through World Law*. Chief Justice Earl Warren delivered an address in Geneva, Switzerland, March 12, 1966, titled "World Peace through Law."[6] World renowned British historians, H.G. Wells and Arnold J. Toynbee, were each advocates of world law. The latter published an article in *The New York Times Magazine*, April 5, 1964, titled "It is One World or No World,"[7] and in 1977, CBS News Anchorman Walter Cronkite wrote in *A Reporter's Life*, "...the world is unlikely to survive a third world war...If we are to avoid that catastrophe, a system of world order—preferably a world government—is mandatory."[8]

President Ronald Reagan addressed the UN General Assembly on September 26, 1983. The content of his address would shock many who identify as his disciples, but it is in keeping with his earlier years as a member of the Democratic Party and the United World Federalists. Here are his words:

President Reagan

Today, at the beginning of this 38th session, I solemnly pledge my nation to upholding the original ideals of the United Nations. Our goals are those that guide this very body. Our ends are the same as the UN's founders, who sought to replace a world at war with one where the rule of law would prevail, where human rights were honored, where development would blossom, where conflict would give way to freedom from violence.[9]

President Bush

President George Herbert Walker Bush, Reagan's successor, openly and proudly touted, "A New World Order," and set forth to make the United Nations work.

In the First Gulf War, when Iraq invaded Kuwait, the Bush administration organized a thirty-four-nation coalition to resist Iraqi aggression. Operating under the authority of unanimous Security Council resolutions, this United Nations coalition efficiently contained Saddam Hussein.

Pushed back within his own country, and controlled by international sanctions and UN inspection teams, Hussein was powerless. Accordingly, the First Gulf War ended quickly with few casualties and minimal, widely shared, expense. President George H. W. Bush had made the UN work. The United States was held in high favor as the nation that led the world to resist aggression and contain Hussein.

As a follow-up to the First Gulf War, on April 13, 1991, President George H. W. Bush addressed the airmen at Maxwell Air Force Base, Montgomery, Alabama. His courageous topic was "The Possibility of a New World Order: Unlocking the Promise of Freedom."[10]

The second President Bush, George W., believed Saddam Hussein was developing a nuclear weapon, so he withdrew UN forces from Iraq and ordered a unilateral, preventive strike. The Second Gulf War brought strikingly inferior results in terms of length of engagement, casualties, war debts, resultant post war problems, and world support.

Bi-Partisan Support

The pursuit of a world security system is not a Republican or Democratic idea. In fact, it was Wendell Willkie, the Republican candidate for president in the election of 1940, who published a national best seller titled *One World*; but the most persistent and dedicated leader for the cause was JFK.

John F. Kennedy's passionate pleas for the pursuit of world law extended from his salad days as a senator to the last week of his life. He was a twentieth-century statesman who had an international vision that extended through the twenty-first century and beyond. In his brief political career, Kennedy supplied plausible answers for the most urgent challenges of our time.

End Notes

[1] Einstein, Albert. "Peace in the Atomic Era," *Vital Speeches of the Day* (March 1, 1950) 302.

[2] Teller, Edward. *The Legacy of Hiroshima* (NY: Doubleday and Company, 1962), 209.

[3] *Public Papers of the Presidents of the United States: Harry S. Truman, Containing the Messages, Statements and Speeches of the President, January 1, 1946 to December 31, 1946.* (Washington, DC: US Government Printing Office, 1962), 39.

[4] *Public Papers of the Presidents of the United States: Dwight D. Eisenhower, Containing the Public Messages, Speeches, and Statements of the President, January 1 to December 31, 1960* (Washington DC: US Government Printing Office, 1961), 707.

[5] *Public Papers of the Presidents of the United States: Dwight D. Eisenhower, Containing the Public Messages, Speeches, and Statements of the President, January 1 to December 31, 1959* (Washington DC: US Government Printing Office, 1960), 18.

[6] Warren, Earl. "World Peace through Law," *Vital Speeches of the Day* (April 15, 1966): 387-90.

[7] Toynbee, Arnold J. "It is One World or No World," *New York Times Magazine* (April 5, 1964). See also "Conditions of Survival" *Saturday Review* (August 29, 1964): 24-26ff.

[8] Cronkite, Walter. *A Reporter's Life: Walter Cronkite* (Alfred A. Knopf, 1997). 128.

[9] *Public Papers of the Presidents of the United States: Ronald Reagan, Containing the Public Messages, Speeches, and Statements of the President. January 1 to December 31, 1983* (Washington, DC: US Government Printing Office, 1985), 1350-54.

[10] Bush, George Herbert Walker. "The Possibility of a New World Order." *Vital Speeches of the Day* (May 15, 1991): 450-52.

CHAPTER FOUR

Uncovering the Kennedy Legacy:
Pursuit of World Law

The media in America have defined President Kennedy as the princely figure of Camelot, the central figure in a murder mystery, the resolute cold warrior, the brave leader with grave health issues—and in terms of his controversial private life. As a result we are on the brink of the 2017 JFK centenary with no clear picture of the central commitment of his administration and no real definition of his legacy.

John F. Kennedy stands in bold relief as a visionary leader. His heroic proposals make most men who have served as president seem timid and tentative.

President Kennedy

In the annals of great historic achievements, Theodore Roosevelt's Panama Canal looms large, Franklin D. Roosevelt's Manhattan Project opened the atomic age, and John F. Kennedy's call for a moon landing opened the era of space travel.

It took enormous vision and courage to call a joint session of Congress on May 25, 1961, and to announce to the country and to the world, the dramatic and ambitious goal of sending a man to the moon and returning him safely to earth before the close of the decade.

Kennedy had campaigned in 1960 on the issue of a missile gap. He shared the embarrassment of many Americans who had been shocked by the Soviet launch of Sputnik, humankind's first unmanned satellite, and later the launch of cosmonaut Yuri Gagarin, the first person to orbit the earth.

JFK responded to the Soviets by assembling the elements and garnering the funds for the Apollo Project—a NASA-backed effort that was able to accomplish his moon mission within his proposed time frame.

On July 16, 1969 Apollo 11 left earth with astronauts Neil Armstrong, Buzz Aldrin, and Michael Collins aboard. Landing on July 20, 1969, Neil Armstrong and Buzz Aldrin spent the next twenty-one hours on the moon. They received a televised long distance telephone call from President Richard Nixon. The president paid tribute to the brave astronauts, and Armstrong responded briefly. Nothing was mentioned about President Kennedy's enormous role in creating this project.

While the two astronauts cavorted on the moon, Michael Collins kept the command module in orbit. Armstrong and Aldrin then rejoined Collins in the command module, splashing down in the Pacific Ocean on July 24, 1969.

The Apollo 11 mission was the first of six American moon landings. In total, twelve American astronauts have walked on the moon, and twenty-four of them have orbited the moon, some in preparation for the first moon landing. Follow-up unmanned exploratory missions to Mars and other planets have been conducted as well. The successful Apollo project is an enormous component of the Kennedy legacy.

Another significant Kennedy achievement was the Peace Corps, which was created by JFK's executive order of March 1, 1961. The Corps was then authorized by Congress on September 21, 1961, for the purpose of promoting peace and helping people to achieve necessary skills for the advancement of their respective societies.

From 1961 to 2013, over 210,000 Americans served needy people in 139 countries as Peace Corps volunteers.

The Pursuit of World Law

Burdened with the tensions of the Cold War, plagued with the residue of terror from the McCarthy era, and hampered by the sham of the John Birch Society, Senator Kennedy faced the extremists of his day with an eloquent speech on disarmament, delivered in Washington DC, on December 11, 1959. Among other things he bravely asserted "It is for us now to meet expectations with far-reaching new plans of our own...We must design and propose a program that combines disarmament with the strengthening of the United Nations." (Doc, I:51)

His second heroic statement came in a speech titled "A New 12-Point Agenda in Foreign Policy," delivered in Washington DC on June 11, 1960. Senator Kennedy's eleventh point was "...we must move toward the eventual rule of world law by working to strengthen the United Nations and to increase its role in resolving international conflicts..." (Doc. II:57).

This twelve-point agenda in foreign policy was widely disseminated as a prominent part of JFK's campaign for the presidency. It was centrally featured in his bestselling book, *The Strategy of Peace.*

These two senatorial speeches seem far too radical for the political climate of the twenty-first century. Modern opinions have been shaped by the anti-United Nations rhetoric that floods our airwaves and appears randomly in print journalism as well.

A Courageous Goal

The next bold stroke by presidential candidate Kennedy and the New Frontiersmen was to publish the following plank regarding the United Nations, in the Democratic Party Platform of 1960:

> *To all our fellow members of the United Nations: We shall strengthen our commitments in this our great, continuing institution for conciliation and the growth of a world community. Through the machinery of the United Nations we shall work for disarmament, the establishment of an international police force, the strengthening of the world court, and the establishment of world law* (Doc. III:65).

Brave words such as these won the day. In the election of 1960, Kennedy defeated Richard Nixon by an electoral margin of 303 to 219, but strong majorities for Nixon in rural areas made the popular vote margin very slim—49.7 percent for Kennedy to 49.5 percent for Nixon.

The Kennedy Inaugural

The heroic centerpiece of the JFK inaugural address was his call for "a grand and global alliance, North, South, East and West against tyranny, poverty, disease, and war itself."

The New York Times summarized the inaugural with this banner headline,

Kennedy Sworn In; Asks Global Alliance
Against Tyranny, Want, Disease, and War.

The headline accurately summarized an address that was twenty-seven paragraphs in length. Virtually all of it dealt with foreign policy matters and international concerns.

Specifically—in paragraph 9, the President pledged to enlarge the area where the UN's "writ may run." In paragraph 15, Kennedy challenged the Soviets, saying, "Let both sides formulate specific and precise proposals for the inspection and control of arms—and bring the absolute power to destroy other nations under the absolute control of all nations." And in Paragraph 18, JFK said, "Let both sides join in creating a new endeavor, not a new balance of power, but a new world of law, where the strong are just and the weak secure and the peace preserved."

The fact is—that JFK's inaugural address boldly emphasized global problems, with the aforementioned references for the need to strengthen the UN and to develop world law.

But three paragraphs from his closing, Kennedy finally departed from his international themes and, with great emphasis, shouted out, "And so my fellow Americans, ask not what your country can do for you, ask what you can do for your country" (Doc IV:67). This is the only line that modern media publicizes. It is also the only part of the address that most Americans can recite.

A Truce to Terror

President Kennedy spoke before the UN General Assembly on September 25, 1961. He admonished the delegates that "mankind must put an end to war or war will put an end to mankind…" And he continued "To destroy arms, however, is not enough. We must create even as we destroy—creating worldwide law and law enforcement even as we outlaw worldwide war and weapons…" He also said, "As we extend the rule of law on earth, so must we extend it to man's new domain—outer space." (Doc.V:71).

In the same address Kennedy gave his most succinct rationale for his agenda when he shouted, "For we far prefer world law in the age of self-determination to world war in the age of mass extermination."

He closed his address with a warning: "Together we shall save our planet, or together we shall perish in its flames. Save it we can—and save it we must" he said, "and then shall we earn the eternal thanks of mankind and, as peacemakers, the eternal blessing of God" (Doc.V:71).

Arms Control and Disarmament

Five days after this address, JFK signed HR 9118, thereby creating the US Arms Control and Disarmament Agency. In his remarks upon signing the bill, he said, "Our ultimate goal, as the act points out, is a world free from war and free from the dangers and burdens of armaments in which the use of force is subordinated to the rule of law, and in which international adjustments to a changing world are achieved peacefully" (Doc VI:83).

The Cuban Missile Crisis

Kennedy inherited a plot from the Eisenhower administration to arm and train Cuban exiles for an invasion of Cuba. The CIA was implementing this plan when Kennedy assumed office. He accepted, authorized, and presided over this "Bay of Pigs" fiasco—an abortive attempt to overthrow the Castro regime.

Convinced that the United States would soon launch a second invasion, Fidel Castro was receptive to Premier Khrushchev's proposal that the Soviet Union should secretly begin to install medium- and intermediate-range nuclear-missile sites in Cuba.

Khrushchev was interested not only in deterring further US attempts to invade Cuba, but also in responding to the US missiles that had been placed in Turkey. He asserted that if the United States could place missiles in a country that shared a border with the USSR, he should be able to place Soviet missiles ninety miles off the US coast.

The Cuban Missile Crisis began on October 15, 1962, when a U2 flight revealed that the building of a Soviet nuclear-missile base was underway in Cuba. Kennedy immediately called together EXCOMM, a group of twelve of his top military and political advisors.

In a thirteen-day session JFK's EXCOMM mulled over proposals to take out the missile sites militarily with a follow-up invasion, but it was finally decided just to blockade Cuba to prevent further delivery of material to the sites. Meanwhile, during the negotiations with the USSR, several Soviet ships tried to cross the blockade, and an American U2 flight over Cuba was shot down. In this atmosphere of high tension, the United States and the Soviet Union came perilously close to nuclear war.

The confrontation ended on October 28, 1962, when it was finally agreed that the Soviet Union would withdraw nuclear missiles from Cuba, and the United States, in turn, would pledge never to invade Cuba again. The United States also agreed to remove missiles from Turkey, but, for political reasons, Kennedy insisted that this American concession was to remain secret.

Communications during the missile crisis were crude and primitive. Both sides soon realized that telegrams were inadequate in the fast-moving events of a nuclear showdown. Therefore, a Washington-Moscow "hot line" was established with a red phone in each high command.

The Cuban Missile Crisis cost Premier Khrushchev his leadership position, and it chastened American leaders as well as the American people. President Kennedy's peace proposals now had a much wider and more receptive audience.

State of the Union

In his third State of the Union message, January 14, 1963, President Kennedy called for an increased defense budget, one that was "about equal to the combined budget of our European allies." He added:

> *But our commitment to national safety is not a commitment to expand our military establishment indefinitely. We do not dismiss disarmament as an idle dream... In this quest the United Nations requires our full and continued support... Today the United Nations is primarily the protector of the small and the weak, and a safety valve for the strong. Tomorrow it can form the framework for a world of law—a world in which no nation dictates the destiny of another, and in which the vast resources now devoted to destructive means will serve constructive ends* (Doc. IX:89).

The Cuban Missile Crisis had sharpened Kennedy's resolve to pursue his quest for peace, but in the spring of 1963 he was preoccupied with many other important public matters. Among these were his $13.6 billion tax-cut proposal, his work with a commission on registration and voting participation (which led to the anti-poll tax and eighteen-year-old voting rights amendments to the Constitution) and his proposal for a domestic service corps, a counterpart to his international Peace Corps. Meanwhile his call for a moon landing within the sixties seemed more feasible by May 16, 1963, when Major L. Gordon Cooper completed a twenty-two-orbit flight around the earth.

Commencement at American University

On June 10, 1963, Kennedy delivered an important commencement address at American University in Washington, DC. Speaking about the Soviet Union, he said:

> *So let us not be blind to our differences, but let us also direct attention to our common interests and to the means by which those differences can be resolved. And if we cannot end now our differences, at least we can help make the world safe for diversity. For in the final analyses our most basic common link is that we all inhabit this planet. We all breathe the same air. We all cherish our children's future. And we are all mortal.*
>
> *Meanwhile we seek to strengthen the United Nations, to help solve its financial problems, to make it a more effective instrument for peace, to develop it into a genuine world security system—a system capable of resolving disputes on the basis of law, of insuring the security of the large and the small, and of creating conditions under which arms can be finally abolished* (Doc. X:91).

A Nuclear Test Ban Treaty

In a television address to the American people on July 26, 1963, President Kennedy said:

> *Yesterday a shaft of light cut into the darkness. Negotiations were concluded in Moscow on a treaty to ban all nuclear tests in the atmosphere, in outer space and under water. For the first time an agreement has been reached in bringing the forces of nuclear destruction under international control—a goal first sought in 1946, when Bernard Baruch presented a comprehensive control plan to the United Nations* (Doc. XI:97).

Stressing the urgency for public support and US Senate ratification, JFK said:

> *A war today or tomorrow, if it led to nuclear war, would not be like any war in history. A full scale nuclear exchange, lasting less than sixty minutes, with the weapons now in existence, could wipe out more than 300 million Americans, Europeans, and Russians, as well as untold numbers elsewhere* (Doc. XI:97).

While Kennedy emphasized nuclear horror and the arms race as a reason for adoption of a nuclear-test ban, that was only part of his rationale. The Nuclear Test Ban Treaty was conceived not only as a curb on the arms race, but more importantly, as a means of ending deadly radioactive fallout in the atmosphere.

Norman Cousins

Norman Cousins and Dr. Linus Pauling had spent years campaigning for a treaty in order to deal with the accumulation of new toxic, human made radioactive elements that were falling out all over the world. As a presidential envoy, Mr. Cousins had also met with Pope John XXIII and Premier Khrushchev, in order to lay important groundwork for JFK's atmospheric ban.

When the treaty was completed, the next step was to obtain Senate ratification.

In his news conference of September 12, 1963, President Kennedy made a strong appeal for public support for US Senate ratification of the treaty. He commended Senator Mike Mansfield (D) of Montana and Senator Everett Dirksen (R) of Illinois for delivering speeches that made a very effective case for ratification. And he added:

> *The treaty will allow all of us who inhabit the earth, our children and children's children, to breathe*

easier, free from the fear of nuclear test fallout. It will curb the spread of nuclear weapons to other countries thereby holding out hope for a more peaceful and stable world. It will slow down the nuclear arms race without impairing the adequacy of this nation's arsenal or security, and it will offer a small but important foundation on which a world of law can be built (Doc. XII:105).

Kennedy and his supporters had triumphed. Public sentiment for an atmospheric-test ban brought Senate ratification on September 24, 1963.

"A Worldwide Program of Conservation"

In the interim, President Kennedy made his last appearance before the United Nations on September 20, 1963. His drive for a strengthened United Nations had reached its zenith. He spoke with pride about how the Sixteenth and Seventeenth General Assemblies had reduced world tensions; he reminded the delegates that the integrity of the Secretariat had been confirmed, the United Nations Decade of Development was underway, and a nuclear-test-ban treaty had been signed by nearly one hundred nations. He said his visit to the UN was not prompted by a crisis, but by confidence: "I have come to salute the United Nations and to show the support of the American people for your daily deliberations."

Citing the serious differences between Americans and Soviets, he also pointed out important areas of agreement and cooperative achievement, and then boldly stated:

But more can be done.

A world center for health communications under the World Health Organization could warn of epidemics, and the adverse effects of certain drugs, as well as transmit the results of new experiments and new discoveries.

Regional research centers could advance our common medical knowledge and train new scientists and doctors for new nations. A global system of satellites could provide communication and weather information for all corners of the earth.

*A worldwide program of conservation could protect
the forests and wild game preserves now in danger of
extinction for all time, improve the harvest of food
from the ocean, and prevent the contamination of air
and water by industrial as well as nuclear pollution*
(Doc. XIII:107).

He also reminded us "the earth, the sea and the air are the concern of
every nation. And science, technology and education can be the ally of
every nation" (Doc. XIII:107).

When Kennedy spoke these words, the Santa Barbara oil spill and the
beginning of environmental consciousness were more than five years
away; ozone depletion was not widely understood; the greenhouse effect
and global warming were not discussed; destruction of the rainforests
was not a concern; nor was the problem of acid rain. Furthermore, Earth
Day had not yet been established. In this context, JFK's preoccupation
with environmental issues and his proposal for a worldwide program of
conservation seems prophetic.

The Kennedy administration resolved the most pressing problem of
atmospheric pollution of that day with the nuclear-test ban of 1963.
Human-produced radioactivity has been virtually eliminated in the
atmosphere as a result.

Given the approach that Kennedy took on environmental issues, it seems
certain that if he were with us today, he would be leading a vigorous
effort to attack the problems of global warming, destruction of rain
forests, acid rain, ozone depletion, and other environmental threats.
There is no doubt that he would still say, fifty years later, that we must
proceed with a worldwide program of conservation.

One World and One Human Race, with One Common Destiny

But the focus, for now, is back to his epic address of September 20, 1963.
Following his proposal for a worldwide conservation program, he
praised the peace-keeping record of the United Nations "in the Congo,
in the Middle East, in Korea and Kashmir, in West New Guinea and
Malaysia. But what the United Nations has done in the past is less
important than the tasks for the future…" He then proceeded to his most
comprehensive rendition of a familiar theme.

The United Nations cannot survive as a static organization. Its obligations are increasing as well as its size. Its charter must be changed as well as its customs. The authors of that charter did not intend that it be frozen in perpetuity. The science of weapons and war has made us all, far more than eighteen years ago in San Francisco, one world and one human race, with one common destiny. In such a world absolute sovereignty no longer assures us of absolute security. The conventions of peace must pull abreast and then ahead of the inventions of war. The United Nations, building on its successes and learning from its failures, must be developed into a genuine world security system (Doc XIII:107).

Address at the University of Maine

On October 19, 1963, President Kennedy addressed the students at the University of Maine. He reminded them that while we were testing nuclear weapons underground and building our stockpile of nuclear weapons, all "elements of American and allied policy were directed at a single comprehensive goal"—to convince the Soviet Union that it could not win through forceful means, and that it would fall to their advantage "to join in the achievement of a genuine and enforceable peace (Doc. XV:119).

Kennedy's legendary thousand days would soon play out with his fateful trip to Dallas, Texas, on November 22, 1963. He had bravely fought for a safer world. He had looked across the world of threats and ventured beyond the conventional sphere of plot and counterplot. He had kept NATO, the free-world defense shield, strong; he had beefed up conventional forces; he had increased our overall capacity in defense; and he had left his nation prepared for any contingency.

On November 18, 1963, Secretary of Defense Robert S. McNamara declared that the West held a commanding military advantage over the Soviet Union in nuclear deterrence and equality in conventional forces.

On November 20, JFK submitted the Seventeenth Annual Report to the Congress of the United States on US Participation in the United Nations. He closed the document with these words:

But despite non-cooperation from some members, and wavering support from others, the organization moved significantly toward the goal of a peace system worldwide in scope. The United States will continue to lend vigorous support to the building of that system (Doc. XVI:121).

On November 22, 1963, "vigorous support for the building of that system" vanished with the assassination of the president.

CHAPTER FIVE

The Ultimate American Triumph:
A World Federal System Based on the American Model

The Voices of Dissent

Objections to the idea of a strengthened United Nations and the development of world law are everywhere. Some say that it is a Quixotic crusade—that it is naïve and impractical. If that is so, what is the alternative pathway of choice? Is there a better survival perspective? Is what we are doing now sophisticated and practical—or even hopeful?

Some say we cannot expect to build a world-security system until all nations subscribe to the same political and cultural values and principles. But isn't it because the world is diverse with so many sharp conflicts—isn't it because the world is so dangerously divided—that we all need to agree on peace and a way to enforce it? Doesn't it make sense to opt for the ultimate social contract, and devise a system to protect pluralism and diversity? And in the process, doesn't it make sense to create ways to preserve and maintain a livable habitat for humankind? Shouldn't America lead the way?

Some say that if Americans try to develop world law, we will lose our sovereignty and our national identity. Some say that such an agenda is un-American. Others say that it is the work of the anti-Christ. But isn't it really the work of patriots who believe that we could check tyranny and promote freedom at the international level?

The starting point for the creation of a world shaped in the American image is a belief that it is possible, that it is desirable, and that it should be attempted.

President Kennedy and most other advocates of the development of world law didn't ever advocate American federalism or any other form of federalism as a model, but they must have had some of the following in mind:

The Case for American Federalism

Ten Salient Points

1. In the tradition of American federalism, world federalism could institutionalize freedom, harbor ideological differences, and foster pluralism and diversity. In President Kennedy's words, the world could be made "safe for diversity."

2. America's federal system of checks and balances could be utilized to curb tyranny at the international level by specifying and limiting the powers granted to the three strengthened branches of the United Nations.

3. The American federal system of division of power between the national government and the states could be adapted in a world system with a division of power between world authority and national authority.

4. World federalism could provide the structure for control of nuclear weapons.

5. World federalism could protect, for all time, the rain forests and other natural habitats that sustain life on earth, just as American federalism has protected millions of acres of national parks and national forest reserve.

6. World federalism could protect freedom just as American federalism has been the protector of freedom. A sacred Bill of Rights is appended to the American Constitution, guaranteeing personal freedoms, civil liberties, and human rights. Under world federalism with the Universal Declaration of Human Rights attached to a revised UN charter, freedoms and civil liberties could be expanded and maintained worldwide (Doc. XVII:125).

7. Under American federalism, slavery was abolished and citizenship and suffrage were extended to former slaves. Suffrage was also extended to all women and all citizens who are eighteen years of age or older. A world federal system could extend freedom, extend suffrage, and otherwise empower world citizens.

8. The American federal government has provided subsidies, grants, contracts, and incentives in order to develop the nation's roads, canals, highways, railroads, and countless features of the national infrastructure. Under world federalism subsidies, contracts and incentives could be awarded to develop hydroelectric-power sites, non-depleting and non-polluting hydrogen as a fuel, solar power, wind power, and other alternatives to destructive fossil fuels.

9. Under American federalism, massive federal spending saved American capitalism in the Great Depression and helped win World War II and the Cold War. Under world federalism, the American government could gain a peace dividend and tap a national tax base that formerly financed enormous defense budgets. New emphasis could be placed on rebuilding cities, repairing and extending federal highways, building new schools, reducing class size, providing professional compensation for teachers, first responders, and other public servants, and subsidizing an industry of alternative fuels.

10. Freedom could flourish if we strengthened the UN Security Council, the General Assembly, and the International Court of Justice, specifying the powers of each branch in a world constitution, thereby creating a system of checks and balances against tyranny. In the best of all possible worlds, the preamble to this world constitution might read:

> We the people of the United Nations of the world, in order to form a more perfect union, establish justice, insure international tranquility, provide for the common defense, promote the general welfare, and

> secure the blessings of liberty to ourselves and our
> posterity, do ordain and establish this Constitution for
> the United Nations of the World.

Liberty could prevail if we were to create and enforce world law based upon the Universal Declaration of Human Rights. Twenty-first-century American patriotism could flourish if a world system based on an American model were in place. If this could be achieved without force or war, it would be the ultimate American triumph.

Kennedy's Grand and Global Alliance:

An Abstract

President John F. Kennedy was a visionary who was preoccupied with the possibility of human survival. His survival perspective was outlined in speeches and statements that extended from his salad days as a senator to the last days of his life. He admonished us to strengthen the United Nations, build a world-security system, develop a worldwide program of conservation, seek world peace through the development of world law, and he set the stage for all of this in his inaugural address, with his eloquent call for "a grand and global alliance."

Kennedy furnished a politics of survival for the twenty-first Century and beyond. He knew that hope for our children is directly connected with the speed with which we discard political minutiae and deal with the possibility of our impending extinction.

The Kennedy legacy has many components. His goal of a moon landing and the establishment of the Peace Corps are prominent among them, but the most important component was his passionate quest for peace through enforceable law on an environmentally viable planet.

The chances for human survival will improve if we revive JFK's New Frontier. Every segment of the professional, religious, and business community should engage in passionate debate on the development of a national survival agenda. Social scientists should engage in the heroic task of exploring survival issues. Much of the research in the social sciences is now focused on matters that will not alter or shape the stream of history or serve any significant purpose in the future of humankind. It is preeminently the time for social scientists to formulate a meaningful international agenda for our new century and an international foundation for the new millennium. Casual tinkering on these matters will not suffice.

New vital questions must be explored:

- If business can become global, why not labor? Why not government?

- Is enforceable law important for cities, states, and nations? Why not for the world?

- Is the quest for global government impractical and naïve? Is it subversive?

- Is crisis-to-crisis improvisation practical and sophisticated? Or are we just tinkering around the edges of huge environmental and thermonuclear threats?

- Is it possible to create collective attitudes that eclipse human promptings—promptings that harken back to tribalism and that now find their fulfillment in the glorification of the nation-state?

- Is it possible to find new ego-involvement and collective identity in the family of man? Or does this quest require an unattainable transcendence of our very nature?

- Is it important to work for a united world? Is it important to design a structure that protects differences?

If we fail to resolve these important questions, and many others, deadly thermonuclear and environmental issues will remain unattended and unresolved.

Heroic leaders of America's greatest generation have left us an American foundation for world order with three branches of international government and a Universal Declaration of Human Rights. It is left for us to accomplish the lesser part.

Freedom could flourish if we modernized and strengthened the United Nations' executive, legislative, and judicial branches, specifying the powers of each branch in a world constitution, thereby creating a system of checks and balances against tyranny.

Liberty could prevail if we created and enforced world law based upon the Universal Declaration of Human Rights. This epic document was ratified on December 10, 1948, by the General Assembly of the United Nations. The vote was forty-eight to zero with seven abstentions, led by the Soviet Union.

The UDHR has become the most translated document in the world. Most new national constitutions, national laws, and recent treaties have been influenced by it.

December 10 has been designated Human Rights Day by the UN General Assembly, but the United States has failed to promote or commemorate the day—or the fiftieth and sixtieth anniversaries of the Universal Declaration of Human Rights.

Twenty-First Century American patriotism could flourish if a world system, based on an American model, were in place.

BIBLIOGRAPHY

This bibliography demonstrates that in Kennedy's time there was bi-partisan support for a rule of law for nations. Presidents, Secretaries of State, and conservative and liberal members of both parties were advocates for the cause.

Books

Andressen, S. and Willy Ostreng, eds. *International Resource Management.* New York: Columbia University Press, 1990.

Aron, Raymond L. *The Great Debate: Theories of Nuclear Strategy.* New York: Doubleday, 1965.

Brower, Michael. *Cool Energy: The Renewable Solution to Global Warming.* Cambridge, Massachusetts: Union of Concerned Scientists, 1990.

Clark, Grenville and Louis B. Sohn. *World Peace Through World Law.* Harvard University Press, 1973.

Commoner, Barry, *et al, Alternative Technologies for Power Production,* New York: Macmillan Information, 1975.

_____. *Making Peace with the Planet,* with bibliography. New York: Pantheon Books, 1990.

_____. *Science and Survival.* New York: Viking Press, 1996.

_____. *The Closing Circle: Nature, Man and Technology.* New York: Knopf, 1971.

Cousins, Norman. *In Place of Folly.* New York: Harper, 1961.

_____. *Who Speaks for Man?* New York: Macmillan, 1953.

Ehrlich, Paul R. *Extinction: The Causes and Consequences of the Disappearances of Species.* New York: Random House, 1981.

_____. and Anne H. Ehrlich. *The Population Explosion.* New York: Simon & Schuster, 1990.

_____. and Richard L. Harriman. *How to be a Survivor.* New York: Ballantine books, 1971.

_____. *The Population Bomb.* New York: Ballantine books, 1968.

_____. *The Science of Ecology.* New York: Macmillan, 1987
.

Einstein, Albert. *Einstein on Peace.* New York: Simon & Schuster, 1960.

Gardner, John F. *The Secret of Peace and the Environmental Crisis.* New York: Myrin Institute, 1978.

Hoffman, Peter. *The Forever Fuel: The Story of Hydrogen.* Boulder, Colorado: Westview Press, 1981.

Kennedy, John F. *The Strategy of Peace.* New York: Harper, 1960.

Kennedy, Robert F. *To Seek a Newer World.* New York: Doubleday, 1968.

Lippman, Morton. *Chemical Contamination in the Human Environment.* New York: Oxford University Press, 1979.

Miller, Morris. *Debt and Environment, Converging Crises.* New York: United Nations, 1991.

Schlesinger, Arthur M., Jr. *A Thousand Days: John F. Kennedy in the White House.* New York: Houghton Mifflin, 1965.

Siever, Raymond, ed. *Energy and Environment: Readings from Scientific American.* San Francisco: W.H. Freeman, 1980.

Sorenson, Theodore C., *Kennedy.* New York: Harper, 1965.

Weiner, Jonathan. *Planet Earth.* New York: Bantam Books, 1986.

_____. *The Next One Hundred Years: Shaping the Fate of Our Living Earth.* New York: Bantam Books, 1991.

Periodicals

"ABA for Rule of Law: Vote Against Connally Amendment," *America,* (September 17, 1960), 103:631-632.

Acheson, Dean. G. "Law and the Growth of the International Community," *U.S. Department of State Bulletin,* (May 5, 1952.), 26: 694-698.

Baldwin, R.N. "What Road to World Government?" *Annals of the American Academy of Political and Social Science,* (July, 1949), 264: 14-19.

Byrnes, James F. "U.S. Views on Charter Review," *U.S. Department of State Bulletin* (November 9, 1953), 29: 649-650.

Chase, Stuart. "Principles for the Nuclear Age," *Saturday Review,* (May 6, 1961), 44:32-33.

Clarke, Grenville. "Need for Total Disarmament Under Enforceable World Law," *Current History,* (August, 1964), 47:93-96.

Cousins, Norman. "Thought for the New Year," proposal for world federalism, *Saturday Review,* (December 24, 1966), 49:28

_____. "What Is World Law?" *Saturday Review,* (August 14, 1965), 48:24-25.

Deub, G.C. "Unused Potential of the World Court," *Foreign Affairs,* (April 1, 1962), 40:463-470.

Douglas, William O. "Law and Survival," *Vital Speeches of the Day,* (April 15, 1965) 400-403

Dulles, John Foster. "Revision of U.N. Charter" *U.S. Department of State Bulletin,* (September 14, 1953) 29:343.

_____. "U.N. Charter Obsolete from the Start," *U.S. News and World Report,* (September 4, 1953), 35:89-91.

_____. "What the U.N. is and Might Be," *New York Times Magazine,* (October 24, 1948), 10.

"Economics and Politics of Arms Reduction: A Symposium," *Bulletin of the Atomic Scientists,* (April, 1964), 20:6-23.

Eichelberger, Clark M. "World Government via the United Nations," *Annals of the American Academy of Political and Social science,* (July, 1949), 264:20-25.

Einstein, Albert. "Peace in the Atomic Era," *Vital speeches of the Day,* (March 1, 1950), 16:302

Eisenhower, Dwight D., and Richard M. Nixon. "Should U.S. Support World law?" *Foreign Policy Bulletin,* (May 15, 1959), 38:132.

_____. "President Expresses Views on World Court and Disarmament," exchange of letters between D.D. Eisenhower and H.H. Humphrey, with bibliography. *U.S. Department of State Bulletin,* January 25, 1960), 42: 128-130.

Etzioni, A. "Gradual Arms Reduction," *Bulletin of the Atomic Scientists,* (October, 1963), 19:30-33.

Fisher, A.S. "United States Presents Views on the Question of General and Complete Disarmament," *U.S. Department of State Bulletin,* (May 11, 1964), 50:756-759.

"For a Worldwide Judiciary—World Peace Through Law Center, Washington, D.C.," *Time,* (May 28, 1965), 85: 62-63.

Fulbright, J.W. "Outlook for Peace: Sovereignty Must Give Way to law," *Vital Speeches of the Day,* (April 1, 1946), 12:358-360.

Goldberg, Arthur J. "Coming of Age of the U.N.," *U.S. Department of State Bulletin,* (October 3, 1966), 55:492-496.

_____. "Rule of Law in an Unruly World," *U.S. Department of State Bulletin,* (June 13, 1966) 54:936-944.

Herter, Christian A. "Rule of Law among Nations," with bibliography. *U.S. Department of State Bulletin,* (August 5, 1957), 37:223-228.

_____. and W.P. Rogers. "Self Judging Aspect of the U.S. Reservation on Jurisdiction of the International Court," *U.S. department of State Bulletin,* (February 15, 1960), 42:227-232.

_____. "United Nations: A Cornerstone of U.S. Foreign Policy," *U.S. Department of State Bulletin,* (October 19, 1959), 41:507-508.

Johnson, Lyndon B. "Direction and Control of Nuclear Power," *U.S. Department of State Bulletin,* (October 5, 1964), 51:458-460.

_____. and Arthur J. Goldberg. "World Peace Through World Law," *U.S. Department of State Bulletin,* (October 4, 1965), 53:542-548.

Kennedy, Robert F. "Support of Senate resolution 179 Will Help Ensure that Nuclear Weapons are Controlled and Ultimately Banished from the Earth." *The Congressional Record: Proceedings and Debates of the 89th Congress, Second Session.* Vol. 112, No. 81 (May 17, 1966), 10281-10290

Kissinger, Henry A. "Arms Control, Inspection, and Surprise Attack," *Foreign Affairs,* (July 1960), 38:557-575.

Lippman, Walter. "Nuclear Age," *Atlantic,* (May, 1962), 209:46-48.

Lodge, Henry C. "Review of the U.N. Charter," *U.S. Department of State Bulletin,* (March, 22, 1954), 30:451-452.

_____. "U.N. Emergency Force, Responsibility of All Members," *U.S. Department of State Bulletin,* (December 21, 1959), 41:919-922.

MacArthur, Douglas. "Can War be Outlawed from the World?" *U.S. News and World Report,* (February 4, 1955), 38:86-88.

Marshall, George C. "Strengthen the United Nations," *Vital Speeches of the Day,* (May 15, 1948), 14:453-455.

"Memorandum to President Truman: Excerpts from the Federalist Papers," *Saturday Review of Literature,* (March 27, 1948), 31:20.

Moley, Raymond. "World Peace by Law," *Newsweek*, (February 22, 1960), 55:108.

Munro, L. "Can the United Nations Enforce Peace?" *Foreign Affairs*, (January, 1960), 38:209-218.

"New Blow at Connaly: U.S. Chamber of Commerce Calls for Repeal of the Connally Reservation," *Time*, (May 7, 1965), 85:24.

"Nixon Champions the Rule of Law," *Life*, (April 27, 1959), 46:36.

"Nixon Urges Greater Use of World Court," *Christian Century*, April 29, 1959), 76:507.

Patterson, E.M. ed. "World Government," *Annals of the American Academy of Political and Social Science*, (July, 1949), 264:1-114.

Phleger, H. "Fifty Years of Progress in International Law," with bibliography. *U.S. Department of State Bulletin*, (April 23, 1956), 34:663-666.

Rhyne, Charles S. "What Law Day Is About," *Life*, (May 11, 1959), 46:32.

Rusk, Dean "Building a Decent World Order," *U.S. Department of State Bulletin*, (July 5, 1965), 53:27-30.

_____. "Nonproliferation of Nuclear weapons," *U.S. Department of State Bulletin*, (March 14, 1966), 54:406-410.

Sohn, L.B. "Security Through Disarmament," *Nation*, (February 25, 1961), 192:159-163.

"Soviets Propose a U.N. Peace Force," *Christian Century*, (July 22, 1964), 81:924.

Stevenson, Adlai E. "American tradition and its Implications for International Law," with bibliography. *U.S. Department of State Bulletin*, (December 11, 1961), 45:959-965.

_____. "Fundamental Meaning of the United Nations: A world of Law and Justice," *Vital Speeches of the Day,* (August 1, 1965), 32:615-617.

_____. "Past, Present and Future of the U.N.," *New York Times Magazine,* (January 14, 1962), 12.

_____. "United Nations: First Step Toward A World Under Law," *U.S. Department of State Bulletin,* (July 10, 1961), 45:68-71.

"Strength for the International Court of Justice," *America,* (February 13, 1960), 102:576.

Taft, Robert A. "Law and Justice: The Base of Peace," *Vital Speeches of the Day*, (October 15, 1947), 14:15-20.

"The Question of Strengthening the United Nations," with pro and con discussion. *Congressional Digest,* (August, 1960), 39:193-224.

"The World Court and the Connally Amendment," with pro and con discussion. *Congressional Digest,* (January, 1961), 40:1-32.

"Toward a Rule of Law," Senator Humphrey's resolution. *New Republic,* (May 9, 1960), 142:5-6.

"Towards a True World Court: Vote to Oppose Connally Reservation by ABA," *Commonweal,* (September 16, 1960), 72:486.

Toynbee, Arnold J. "Conditions of Survival," *Saturday Review,* (August 29, 1964), 47:24-26+.

_____. "It Is One World or No World," *New York Times Magazine,* (April 5, 1964), 28.

Truman, Harry S. "From USA to USW?" President Truman's call for transformation of the U.N. into a world government. *Christian Century,* (February 6, 1946), 63:166-168.

_____. "United Nations: Cornerstone of U.S. Foreign Policy," *U.S. Department of State Bulletin,* (October 6, 1952), 27:529.

"USA and World Federation," pro and con discussion. *Congressional Digest,* (August, 1952), 31:193-224.

Warren, Earl. "World Peace through Law," *Vital Speeches of the Day,* (April 15, 1966), 387-390.

Welles, Sumner. "The Atomic Bomb and world Government," *Atlantic,* (January, 1946), 177:39-42.

"What We Are For: Summary of New Encyclical on World Peace," by Pope John XXIII, *Time,* (April 19, 1963), 81:60+.

Appendix

Document I

Senator John F. Kennedy

DISARMAMENT*

An Address Delivered at Washington, D.C.
December 11, 1959

No sane society chooses to commit national suicide. Yet that is the fate which the arms race has in store for us-unless we can find a way to stop it.

There is some argument as to just what proportion of our population would be destroyed in a missile-megaton war in the next decade. But having recently attended hearings at which scientists and experts were testifying-in that detached, statistical manner that scientists have-about what would happen to this country and the world if war should come. I am sorry to say that there is too much point to the wisecrack that life is extinct on other planets because their scientists were more advanced than ours. Already our total destructive capacity is sufficient to annihilate the enemy twenty-five times over-he has the power to destroy us ten times. Between us we are in a position to exterminate all human life seven times over. The nuclear load in only one of our B-52's now in the air at this minute somewhere above us or over the Arctic-is said to be greater in terms of destructive power than all of the explosives used in all of the previous wars in human history. Yet today our hopes are still dim that any proposals for universal disarmament will be agreed upon by either the U.S. or the U.S.S.R. Disarmament remains a pious phrase which both sides invoke but which they will not implement together. It is often said that arms are only a symptom of tension, not the cause of it; and that, so long as situations such as Berlin exist, it will be necessary to continue the arms race. But this is at best a half-truth.

Atomic and hydrogen weapons themselves have become a major source of tension. Behind many political conflicts lie problems of the military balance of power - problems rising from the need to maintain troops or

---

*Alan Nevins, (ed.) Senator John F. Kennedy: *The Strategy of Peace.* (New York: Harper and Brothers, 1960).

air bases or nuclear missile installations problems that would not arise outside the context of the arms race.

The truth is that we are caught in a vicious circle comprised in part of the arms race and in part of political conflict. For us, this vicious circle of two great powers contending with each other for sway over the destiny of man is compounded by the new dynamics of an expansive world Communism, armed with revolutionary doctrines of class warfare and modern methods of subversion and terror. For the Kremlin, this struggle for the world is complicated by the contagious quality of freedom-by the ferment within the Communist empire for the freedom that all men want-by the powerful example and contrast that America and other free lands present to people suffering under Communist conformity. Yet both sides in this fateful struggle must come to know, sooner or later, that the price of running this arms race to the end is death-for both.

Some historic vicious circles have simply worn down and petered out in time. Toynbee keeps hopefully recalling that the cold and hot wars waged by a fanatic Islam and a crusading Christendom gradually transformed themselves into centuries of perpetual truce, although both parties retained their universal goals. Communism and the West, he suggests, may in time come tacitly to agree to coexist, even while each hopes and works for the extension of its way of life to the whole world.

The trouble with this cheerful picture is that the pace of events is much faster now-the logic of the present arms race seems to require more of a collision course than the slow changes wrought in medieval times. .In the days of the crusades, it took months sometimes years--of sailing by sea and marching overland for two worlds to collide. Today the deadly missiles with hydrogen warheads are only minutes away. For the first time since the War of 1812, the American people live on what would be the front lines of a world war. In 1814, forty British vessels outside Baltimore Harbor fired two-hundred-pound balls for twenty-five hours. "An awful spectacle to behold," Bishop John Carroll wrote. But it was nothing like the spectacle of a city going up in a nuclear cloud from one hydrogen bomb launched from one Soviet submarine. Today our cities are the bull's-eye of the Soviet missile targets, just as their cities are the targets of our Strategic Air Force. To prevent this conflagration, some dramatic intervention is required to break the vicious circle of the Cold War and to start a constructive circle of confidence.

Since the circle of fear is fed both by the arms race itself and by the political conflicts between the West and the Communist world, real progress on either part of the problem—on either a political settlement of some important outstanding issue, or on atomic control and disarmament-might suffice to start a momentum toward peace, toward the kind of agreement to live and inhabit the same planet (even while disagreeing about other things) that Toynbee foresees. In this formula, progress on either problem must lead to progress on the other if the source of the vicious circle is to be controlled. It is with this in mind that we must press forward now for any practical disarmament agreement within reach-not as a substitute for efforts to settle some of the great political divisions such as Germany, Korea, Vietnam, or China, but as a way of moving these and all other problems back from the brink of war. The way for these problems to be resolved-the only way now open-is through the peaceful processes of history that Toynbee describes. Our job is to bring those processes into play quickly, even though the ultimate resolution may take generations—or even centuries.

Some say that there is little point in negotiating with the Russians in these terms because they have never abided by any agreement and never will. But this is another way of saying that war is the unavoidable fate of mankind. Lenin used to say this, in the days before war meant the annihilation of whole peoples. Stalin blindly said it, even after the atomic bomb had been dropped on Japan. No American should say it. We who believe in human reason and in the possibilities of peaceful change should never lose hope that even a tough-minded Kremlin politician will see the light—or enough of the light to know that war, in the age of the hydrogen bomb, is no longer a rational alternative.

There are, I say, grounds for hope. We should certainly not neglect our armaments in the meantime. And we must not let our wishes father false thoughts- of unilateral disarmament, of disarmament without adequate controls, or without guarantees that all parties are in fact disarming. But we should not let our fears hold us back from pursuing our hopes. Disarmament talks historically fail when nations refuse to trust each other's intentions enough to take the first step. Even that first step must be subject to adequate inspection and enforcement. But this, too, requires a minimum of trust.

When I say "trust," I do not mean that we should for one moment think that the Kremlin has abandoned its aim of world domination or is ready to disband its present empire. Nor do I ask the Kremlin to think that we of the west have abandoned our concern for the people under Communist domination or our desire to promote the peaceful liberation of all people. But assuming we each maintain these objectives, we can also come to an understanding that peace is the pre-condition for any of these efforts. Naturally each side will assume his own success in the competition. Mr. Khrushchev has left no doubt of his self-confidence-and I am equally confident that, in conditions of peace, we can see freedom thrive and spread-even someday to Mr. Khrushchev's grandchildren. But trust we must-in each other's rational recognition of self-interest-in our mutual self-interest in survival.

The problem is to find a beginning. Archimedes is supposed to have said: "Give me a fulcrum and I can move the world." What we need is the first fulcrum in this situation. In the search for this we need to try every practical possibility.

It may be that an agreement on the control and limitation of nuclear tests will be the beginning if the difficulties of detection and inspection prove insurmountable for the time being on underground or high-atmosphere tests, at least a beginning may be made with an agreement to suspend permanently low-atmosphere testing, which can be monitored adequately and which causes the worst fall-out. Perhaps a U.N. system of inspection to warn against surprise attacks will be acceptable as a start. Or the beginning might be an agreement to explore space jointly under United Nations auspices, perhaps through a world space agency.

Another dramatic step that might reverse the present pattern would be an agreement on general disarmament and demilitarization for some particular area of tension. The treaty of peace and the neutralization of Austria in return for the withdrawal of Soviet occupation forces may point to other applications of such a policy. The Middle East might be an area where a political settlement and disarmament could be fruitfully combined. The new treaty on Antarctica may show the way. Developing techniques of inspection and control in one such area could lead to the extension of these techniques to other areas, and eventually perhaps the world. Out of the experience of the emergency U.N. force sent to Suez could come the nucleus of the work policing forces necessary to ensure such demilitarized zones.

Peace may come through a combination of such beginnings, each small and insufficient in itself but together enough to provide the new momentum.

In this search for beginnings we must bring into play the imagination which our fears have in recent years paralyzed. The initiative taken by the new chairman of the Atomic Energy Commission, John McCone, is an example of the affirmative approach now required. So far it has met with an affirmative Soviet response. Mr. McCone and the United States scientific mission to the Soviet Union were shown far more of Soviet installations and laboratories for peaceful uses of atomic energy than anyone a year ago would have believed possible. And after the Soviet mission here, an initial agreement for co-operation in this field was reached, with far more extensive co-operation now being considered. Here is another beginning that would never have been possible if the negative, ever-suspicious spirit of Mr. McCone's predecessor had continued to prevail.

Even Mr. Khrushchev's all too general proposals for universal disarmament should be explored as a possible beginning, not shunted off as mere propaganda. The Soviet-American agreement and joint resolution in the U.N. Assembly to resume disarmament negotiations and to consider Mr. Khrushchev's proposal was a constructive response--one all too rarely seen. For the lesson to be drawn from Mr. Khrushchev's address to the U.N. was not the inadequacy of his plan-not his lack of specifics on the crucial questions of inspection and control. That was not news. The lesson rather was to be found in the great expectations raised throughout the world by the prospect of the Soviet leader proposing a far-reaching disarmament plan and in the considerable disappointment that his proposal did not go far enough.

It is for us now to meet these expectations with far-reaching new plans of our own, and not to disappoint the world by treating this problem merely as a matter of psychological warfare. We must design and propose a program that combines disarmament with the strengthening of the United Nations and with world development. We must propose the creation of new United Nations institutions of inspection and control and of economic development. And we must demonstrate our good faith by being prepared to make a beginning at any hopeful place along the broad front of present possibilities. So far we have lacked the vision to present a comprehensive program for the development of a world community under law and we have lacked the courage to try small beginnings. The legacy of these years of Cold War that Stalin forced upon us is that our policy-makers on too many levels and in too many fields have become narrow, cautious, and, in the literal sense, reactionary. It is time to stop reacting to our adversary's moves, and to start acting like the bold, hopeful, inventive people that we were born to be, ready to build and begin anew, ready to make a reality of man's oldest dream, world peace.

Document II

Senator John F. Kennedy

A NEW TWELVE-POINT AGENDA IN FOREIGN POLICY*

Address Delivered at Washington, D.C.

June 14, 1960

May 17, 1960 marked the end of an era—an era of illusion—the illusion that platitudes and slogans are a substitute for strength and planning—the illusion that personal good will is a substitute for hard, carefully prepared bargaining on concrete issues—the illusion that good intentions and pious principles are a substitute for strong creative leadership.

For on May 17, 1960, the long-awaited, highly publicized summit conference collapsed. That collapse was the direct result of Soviet determination to destroy the talks. The insults and distortions of Mr. Khrushchev—the violence of his attacks—shocked all Americans and united the country in admiration for the dignity and self-control of President Eisenhower. Regardless of party, all of us deeply resented Russian abuse of this nation and its President—and all of us shared a common disappointment at the failure of the conference. But it is imperative, nevertheless, that we as a nation rise above our resentment and frustration to a critical re-examination of the events at Paris and their meaning for America.

I do not now intend to rehash the sorry story of the U-2 incident, and the image of confusion and indecision which our Government presented to the American people and the world. The Senate Foreign Relations Committee has raised, in a constructive manner, the questions which must be raised, if we are to profit from the unfortunate experience. Nor do I wish to exaggerate the long-range importance of the U-2 incident or the Khrushchev attacks in Paris.

---

*U.S. Congressional Record: Proceedings and Debates of the 86th Congress, Second Session, Vol. 106, Part 10, June 14, 1960 to June 22, 1960 (Washington DC: US Government Printing Office, 1960), 12523-26.

For the harsh facts of the matter are that the effort to eliminate world tensions and end the cold war through a summit meeting—necessary as such an effort was to demonstrate America's willingness to seek peaceful solutions-was doomed to failure long before the U-2 ever fell on Soviet soil. This effort was doomed to failure because we have failed for the past eight years to build the positions of long-term strength essential to successful negotiation. It was doomed because we were unprepared with new policies or new programs for the settlement of outstanding substantive issues. It was doomed because the Soviet Union knew it had more to gain from the increasing deterioration of America's world position than from any concessions that might be made in Paris. Only Mr. Khrushchev's intransigence and violent temper saved the United our friends nor our States from an embarrassing exposure of our inability to make the summit meaningful…..

The hour is late-but the agenda is long.

First—We must make invulnerable a nuclear retaliatory power second to none-by making possible now a stop-gap air alert and base dispersal program—and by stepping up development and production of the ultimate missiles that can close the gap and will not be wiped out in a surprise attack—Polaris, Minuteman and long-range air-to-ground missiles—meanwhile increasing our production of Atlas missiles, hardening our bases and improving our continental defense and warning systems. As a power which will never strike first, we require a retaliatory capacity based on hidden, moving or invulnerable weapons in such force as to deter any aggressor from threatening an attack he knows could not destroy enough of our force to prevent his own destruction. And we must also critically re-examine the far-flung overseas base structure on which much of our present retaliatory strength is based. We must contribute to the political and economic stability of the nations in which our vital bases are located—and develop alternative plans for positions which may become untenable.

Second—We must regain the ability to intervene effectively and swiftly in any limited war anywhere in the world—augmenting, modernizing and providing increased mobility and versatility for the conventional forces and weapons of the Army and Marine Corps. As long as those forces lack the necessary airlift and sealift capacity and versatility of firepower, we cannot protect our commitments around the globe—resist non-nuclear aggressions—or be certain of having enough time to decide on the use of our nuclear power.

Third—We must rebuild NATO into a viable and consolidated military force, capable of deterring any kind of attack, unified in weaponry and responsibility. Aiming beyond a narrow military alliance united only by mutual fears, a return to mutual consultation and respect—and a determined American effort to create a free world economy—can help overcome schismatic economic rivalries between the Continent and Britain, and the Common Market and the "Outer Seven," as well as other Western differences in military and political policy. We need a common effort to protect vital international reserves, to adopt more consistent tariff policies on both sides of the Atlantic and to merge Western contributions to the under-developed areas.

Fourth—We must, in collaboration with Western Europe and Japan, greatly increase the flow of capital to the under-developed areas of Asia, Africa, the Middle East and Latin America—frustrating the Communist hopes for chaos in those nations—enabling emerging nations to achieve economic as well as political independence—and closing the dangerous gap that is now widening between our living standards and theirs. Above all, it is vital that we aid India to make a success of her new five-year program—a success that will enable her to compete with Red China for economic leadership of all Asia. And we must undertake this effort in a spirit of generosity motivated by a desire to help our fellow citizens of the world—not as narrow bankers or self-seeking politicians. Our present foreign aid programs have neglected the great, visionary, partnership principles of the Marshall Plan and Point Four—they have been subordinated to narrow, expedient ends—money has been poured into military assistance programs at the expense of vitally necessary economic development. The next President will have to devise an entirely revamped foreign aid program—a program which will make the long-term commitments essential to successful planning—a program whose administration will not be hampered by waste and mismanagement, or by unsympathetic and unqualified administrators. And part of this program must be a new and expanded effort to use our food surpluses to feed the world's hungry—storing them in "food banks" abroad.

Fifth—We must reconstruct our relations with the Latin American democracies—bringing them into full Western partnership—working through a strengthened Organization of American States—increasing the flow of technical assistance, development capital, private investment, exchange students and agricultural surpluses, perhaps through the large-scale "Operation Pan-America," which has been proposed by the President of Brazil—and pursuing practical agreements for stabilizing commodity prices, trade routes and currency convertibility. A return to the "Good Neighbor Policy" is not enough—dollar diplomacy is not enough—a patronizing attitude taking for granted their dedication to an anti-Communist crusade is not enough. We will need a whole new set of attitudes and emphases to make the nations of Latin America full partners in the rapid development of the Western Hemisphere.

Sixth—We must formulate, with both imagination and restraint, a new approach to the Middle East—not pressing our case so hard that the Arabs feel their neutrality and nationalism are threatened, but accepting those forces and seeking to help channel them along constructive lines, while at the same time trying to hasten the inevitable Arab acceptance of the permanence of Israel. We must give our support to programs to help people instead of regimes—to work in terms of their problems, not ours—and seek a permanent settlement among Arabs and Israelis based not on an armed truce but on mutual self-interest. Guns and anti-Communist pacts and propaganda and the traditional piecemeal approach are not enough—refugee resettlement and a regional resources development fund in full partnership with the Middle Eastern nations, all are parts of a long-range strategy which is both practical and in the best interests of all concerned.

Seventh—We must greatly increase our efforts to encourage the newly emerging nations of the vast continent of Africa—to persuade them that they do not have to turn to Moscow for the guidance and friendship they so desperately need—to help them achieve the economic progress on which the welfare of their people and their ability to resist Communist subversion depend. We can no longer afford policies which refuse to accept the inevitable triumph of nationalism in Africa—the inevitable end of colonialism—or the unyielding determination of the new African states to lift their people from their age-old poverty and hunger and ignorance. We must answer the critical African need for educated men to build the factories, run the schools and staff the governments by sending a growing stream of technical experts and educators to Africa—and by bringing far greater numbers of African students—future African leaders—to our own universities for training. Agricultural experts must be sent into areas where the land is unproductive and where modern methods of agriculture are unknown in order to raise subsistence levels of farming and ensure adequate supplies of food and while this is being done we must use our own food surpluses to prevent hunger. We must establish a multi-nation economic development loan fund—a full working partnership between the nations of the West and the nations of Africa—to provide the capital necessary to start African economic growth on its way. And finally, if our policies toward Africa are to be effective, we must extend this aid in terms of America's desire to bring freedom and prosperity to Africa—not in terms of a narrow self-interest which seeks only to use African nations as pawns in the cold war.

Eighth—We must plan a long-range solution to the problems of Berlin. We must show no uncertainty over our determination to defend Berlin— but we must realize that a solution to the problems of that beleaguered city is only possible in the context of a solution of the problems of Germany and, indeed, the problems of all Europe. We must look forward to a free Berlin, in a united Germany in a Europe where tensions and armaments have been reduced—where perhaps the suggestions of General de Gaulle and Premier Adenauer requiring Soviet withdrawal behind the Urals can be accepted. Such a solution is far from a reality— but both our good faith and our will to resist are dependent on our willingness to face the total problem of tension and conflict in Europe. We must remain precise in our determination to meet our commitments until a change in Soviet policy permits a constructive solution. In the meantime, we should explore how the moral authority of the U.N. could be used to strengthen the security presently provided to the people of West Berlin.

Ninth—We must prepare and hold in readiness more flexible and realistic tools for use in Eastern Europe. The policy of "liberation," proudly proclaimed eight years ago, has proved to be a snare and a delusion. The tragic uprisings in East Germany, in Poland and in Hungary demonstrated clearly that we had neither the intention nor the capacity to liberate Eastern Europe—and the false hopes raised by our promises were cruelly crushed. We must now begin to work slowly and carefully toward programs designed to wean from their Soviet masters any dependents showing signs of discontent—to nourish the seeds of liberty in any cracks appearing in the Iron Curtain by reducing economic and ideological dependence on Russia. There are already opportunities in Poland for greater American initiative, aid, trade, tourism, information services, student and teacher exchanges, and the use of our capital and technology to advance the standard of living of the Polish people. Closer relationships can be offered in other so-called captive nations as well— showing a creative interest, not a closed mind, by the nation that represents their one great hope for freedom.

Tenth—We must reassess a China policy which has failed dismally to move toward its principal objective of weakening Communist rule in the mainland—a policy which has failed to prevent a steady growth in

Communist strength—and a policy which offers no real solution to the problems of a militant China. We need to formulate proposals for a reduction of tension in the Formosa Straits—at the same time making clear our determination to defend that island. We must act through an Asian regional development organization to stabilize the nations of non-Communist Asia both politically and economically, so as to strengthen their resistance to Communist pressures. And, although we should not now recognize Red China or agree to its admission to the United Nations without a genuine change in her belligerent attitude toward her Asian neighbors and the world—and regrettably there is evidence that her belligerence is rising rather than receding—we must nevertheless work to improve at least our communications with mainland China. Perhaps a way could be found to bring the Chinese into the nuclear test ban talks at Geneva—so that the Soviets could not continue their atomic tests on the mainland of China without inspection—and because Chinese possession of atomic weapons could drastically alter the balance of power. If that contact proves fruitful, further cultural and economic contact could be tried, For only in this way can we inform ourselves of Communist activities, attempt to restore our historic friendship with the Chinese people, and make sure that we are not plunged into war by a Chinese miscalculation of our determination to defend all of free Asia. Today we have no affirmative policies—only an attitude of negative resistance—with the chance of dangerous action stemming from mutual miscalculations growing. This cannot last in a world where the Red Chinese are increasingly important, increasingly menacing and increasingly impossible to omit from effective international agreements on subjects such as arms control.

Eleventh—We must begin to develop new, workable programs for peace and the control of arms. We have been unwilling to plan for disarmament, and unable to offer creative proposals of our own, always leaving the initiative in the hands of the Russians. An arms control research institute could undertake the technical studies needed before we can detect and monitor the vast and complex weapons systems of modern warfare. The entire world hopes that the collapse at the summit has not destroyed man's hope for a nuclear test ban, But if such a ban is achieved, it must only be the first step toward halting the spiraling arms race that burdens the entire world with a fantastic financial drain, excessive military establishments, and the chance of an accidental or irrational triggering of a world-wide holocaust. At the same time we must move toward the eventual rule of world law by working to strengthen the United Nations and to increase its role in resolving international conflicts and planning for international scientific and economic development.

Twelfth and finally—We must work to build the stronger America on which our ultimate ability to defend the free world depends. We must increase our own scientific effort—not only by strengthening and revamping existing research programs in all fields, including the exploration of space—but by building an educational system which can produce the talent and skill on which our future strength and progress depend. We must work to create an America with an expanding economy, where growth is not dissipated in inflation, and consumer luxuries are not confused with national strength—an economy capable of supporting our massive needs and our new programs. And we must also work to create an America of equal opportunity and economic justice for all men of all ages, races and creeds—an America which will be, as the founding fathers intended us to be, a living example of freedom to the world.

This is a large agenda—a challenging agenda—and yet I do not pretend that it is, in any sense, complete. For if there is one certain thing in a world of change, it is that the coming years will bring new problems, undreamt of challenges, unanticipated opportunities.

The next President will confront a task of unparalleled dimensions. But this task will not be his alone. For just as he must offer leadership and demand sacrifices—it is the American people who must be willing to respond to these demands.

I realize also that the length of this agenda is in sharp contrast with the rosy assurances of the Administration. "America is today," the Vice President told his national committee Saturday, summarizing our position in the world, "the strongest country militarily, the strongest country economically, with the best educational system [and] the finest scientists in the world, over all." To feed that kind of diet to the American people during the coming months—to confine our national posture to one of talking louder and louder while carrying a smaller and smaller stick—is to trade the long-range needs of the nation for the short-term appearance of security.

For all America—its President and its people—the coming years will be a time of decision. We must decide whether we have reached our limit—whether our greatness is past—whether we can go no further—or whether, in the words of Thomas Wolfe, "the true discovery of America is before us—the true fulfillment of our mighty and immortal land is yet to come."

Document III

THE PLATFORM REFLECTS THE VIEWS OF CANDIDATE JOHN F. KENNEDY

Excerpt from the Democratic Party Platform of 1960

THE UNITED NATIONS*

To all our fellow members of the United Nations: We shall strengthen our commitments in this, our great continuing institution for conciliation and the growth of a world community.

Through the machinery of the United Nations, we shall work for disarmament, the establishment of an international police force, the strengthening of the World Court, and the establishment of world law.

We shall propose the bolder and more effective use of the specialized agencies to promote the world's economic and social development.

Great Democratic Presidents have taken the lead in the effort to unite the nations of the world in an international organization to assure world peace with justice under law.

The League of Nations, conceived by Woodrow Wilson, was doomed by Republican defeat of United States participation.

The United Nations, sponsored by Franklin Roosevelt, has become the one place where representatives of the rival systems and interests which divide the world can and do maintain continuous contact.

The United States' adherence to the World Court contains a so-called "self- judging reservation" which, in effect, permits us to prevent a Court decision in any particular case in which we are involved. The Democratic Party proposes its repeal.

To all these endeavors so essential to world peace, we, the members of the Democratic Party, will bring a new urgency, persistence, and

---

*The Democratic Party Platform of 1960. Online by Gerhard Peters and John T. Wooley, The American Presidency Project. http://www.presidency. ucsb.edu/ws/index.php?pid=29602

determination, born of the conviction that in our thermonuclear century all of the other Rights of Man hinge on our ability to assure man's right to peace.

Document IV

President John F. Kennedy

A GRAND AND GLOBAL ALLIANCE*

Excerpt from the Inaugural Address

January 20, 1961

To that world assembly of sovereign states, the United Nations, our last best hope in an age where the instruments of war have far outpaced the instruments of peace, we renew our pledge of support—to prevent it from becoming merely a forum for invective—to strengthen its shield of the new and the weak—and to enlarge the area in which its writ may run.

Finally, to those nations who would make themselves our adversary, we offer not a pledge but a request: that both sides begin anew the quest for peace, before the dark powers of destruction unleashed by science engulf all humanity in planned or accidental self-destruction.

We dare not tempt them with weakness. For only when our arms are sufficient beyond doubt can we be certain beyond doubt that they will never be employed.

But neither can two great and powerful groups of nations take comfort from our present course-both sides overburdened by the cost of modern weapons, both rightly alarmed by the steady spread of the deadly atom, yet both racing to alter that uncertain balance of terror that stays the hand of mankind's final war.

So let us begin anew—remembering on both sides that civility is not a sign of weakness, and sincerity is always subject to proof. Let us never negotiate out of fear. But let us never fear to negotiate.

Let both sides explore what problems unite us instead of belaboring those problems which divide us.

---

*Public Papers of the Presidents of the United States: John F. Kennedy. Containing the Messages, Speeches and Statements of the President. January 20 to December 31, 1961 (Washington DC: US Government Printing Office, 1962), 2.

Let both sides, for the first time, formulate serious and precise proposals for the inspection and control of arms—and bring the absolute power to destroy other nations under the absolute control of all nations.

Let both sides seek to invoke the wonders of science instead of its terrors. Together let us explore the stars, conquer the deserts, eradicate disease, tap the ocean depths and encourage the arts and commerce. Let both sides unite to heed in all corners of the earth the command of Isaiah—to "undo the heavy burdens and let the oppressed go free."

And if a beachhead of cooperation may push back the jungles of suspicion, let both sides join in creating a new endeavor—not a new balance of power, but a new world of law, where the strong are just and the weak secure and the peace preserved.

All this will not be finished in the first hundred days. Nor will it be finished in the first thousand days, nor in the life of this Administration, nor even perhaps in our lifetime on this planet. But let us begin.

In your hands, my fellow citizens, more than mine, will rest the final success or failure of our course. Since this country was founded, each generation of Americans has been summoned to give testimony to its national loyalty. The graves of young Americans who answered the call to service surround the globe.

Now the trumpet summons us again—not as a call to bear arms though arms we need—not as a call to battle, though embattled we are—but a call to bear the burden of a long twilight struggle, year in and year out, "rejoicing in hope, patient in tribulation"—a struggle against the common enemies of man: tyranny, poverty, disease and war itself.

Can we forge against these enemies a grand and global alliance, north and south, east and west, that can assure a more fruitful life for all mankind? Will you join in that historic effort?

In the long history of the world, only a few generations have been granted the role of defending freedom in its hour of maximum danger. I do not shrink from this responsibility—I welcome it. I do not believe that any of us would exchange places which we bring to this endeavor will light our country and all who serve it—and the glow from that fire can truly light the world.

And so, my fellow Americans: ask not what your country can do for you—ask what you can do for your country.

My fellow citizens of the world: ask not what America will do for you, but what together we can do for the freedom of man.

Finally, whether you are citizens of America or citizens of the world, ask of us here the same high standards of strength and sacrifice which we ask of you. With a good conscience our only sure reward, with history the final judge of our deeds, let us go forth to lead the land we love, asking His blessing and His help, but knowing that here on earth God's work must truly be our own.

Document V

President John F. Kennedy

A TRUCE TO TERROR

Address before the General Assembly of the United Nations

September 25, 1961[1]*

We meet in an hour of grief and challenge. Dag Hammarskjold is dead. But the United Nations lives. His tragedy is deep in our hearts, but the task for which he died is at the top of our agenda. A noble servant of peace is gone. But the quest for peace lies before us.

The problem is not the death of one man—the problem is the life of this organization. It will either grow to meet the challenges of our age, or it will be gone with the wind, without influence, without force, without respect. Were we to let it die, to enfeeble its vigor, to cripple its powers, we would condemn our future.

For in the development of this organization rests the only true alternative to war—and war appeals no longer as a rational alternative. Unconditional war can no longer lead to unconditional victory. It can no longer serve to settle disputes. It can no longer concern the great powers alone. For a nuclear disaster, spread by wind and water and fear, could well engulf the great and the small, the rich and the poor, the committed and the uncommitted alike. Mankind must put an end to war-or war will put an end to mankind. So let us here resolve that Dag Hammarskjold did not live, or die, in vain. Let us call a truce to terror. Let us invoke the blessings of peace. And, as we build an international capacity to keep peace, let us join in dismantling the national capacity to wage war.

This will require new strength and new roles for the United Nations. For disarmament without checks is but a shadow—and a community without law is but a shell. Already the United Nations has become both the measure and the vehicle of man's most generous impulses. Already it has

*Public Papers of the Presidents of the United States: John F. Kennedy. Containing Messages, Speeches and Statements of the President, January 20 to December 31, 1961 (Washington DC: U S Government Printing Office, 1962), 615-26.

provided—in the Middle East, in Asia, in Africa this year in the Congo—a means of holding man's violence within bounds.

But the great question which confronted this body in 1945 is still before us: whether man's cherished hopes for progress and peace are to be destroyed by terror and disruption, whether the "foul winds of war" can be tamed in time to free the cooling winds of reason, and whether the pledges of our Charter are to be fulfilled or defied—pledges to secure peace, progress, human rights and world law.

In this Hall, there are not three forces, but two. One is composed of those who are trying to build the kind of world described in Articles I and II of the Charter. The other, seeking a far different world, would undermine this organization in the process.

Today of all days our dedication to the Charter must be maintained. It must be strengthened first of all by the selection of an outstanding civil servant to carry forward the responsibilities of the Secretary General—a man endowed with both the wisdom and the power to make meaningful the moral force of the world community. The late Secretary General nurtured and sharpened the United Nations' obligation to act. But he did not invent it. It was there in the Charter. It is still there in the Charter.

However difficult it may be to fill: Mr. Hammarskjold's place, it can better be filled by one man rather than by three. Even the three horses of the Troika did not have three drivers, all going in different directions. They had only one—and so must the United Nations executive. To install a triumvirate, or any panel, or any rotating authority, in the United Nations administrative offices would replace order with anarchy, action with paralysis, confidence with confusion.

The Secretary General, in a very real sense, is the servant of the General Assembly. Diminish his authority and you diminish the authority of the only body where all nations, regardless of power, are equal and sovereign. Until all the powerful are just, the weak will be secure only in the strength of this Assembly.

Effective and independent executive action is not the same question as balanced representation. In view of the enormous change in membership in this body since its founding, the American delegation will join in any effort for the prompt review and revision of the composition of United Nations bodies.

But to give this organization three drivers—to permit each great power to decide its own case, would entrench the Cold War in the headquarters of peace.

Whatever advantages such a plan may hold out to my own country, as one of the great powers, we reject it. For we far prefer world law, in the age of self-determination, to world war, in the age of mass extermination.

Today, every inhabitant of this planet must contemplate the day when this planet may no longer be habitable. Every man, woman and child lives under a nuclear sword of Damocles, hanging by the slenderest of threads, capable of being cut at any moment by accident or miscalculation or by madness. The weapons of war must be abolished before they abolish us.

Men no longer debate whether armaments are a symptom or a cause of tension. The mere existence of modem weapons—ten million times more powerful than any that the world has ever seen, and only minutes away from any target on earth—is a source of horror, and discord and distrust. Men no longer maintain that disarmament must await the settlement of all disputes—for disarmament must be a part of any permanent settlement. And men may no longer pretend that the quest for disarmament is a sign of weakness—for in a spiraling arms race, a nation's security may well be shrinking even as its arms increase.

For 15 years this organization has sought the reduction and destruction of arms. Now that goal is no longer a dream—it is a practical matter of life or death. The risks inherent in disarmament pale in comparison to the risks inherent in an unlimited arms race.

It is in this spirit that the recent Belgrade Conference—recognizing that this is no longer a Soviet problem or an American problem, but a human problem—endorsed a program of "general, complete and strictly an internationally controlled disarmament." It is in this same spirit that we in the United States have labored this year, with a new urgency, and with a new, now statutory agency fully endorsed by the Congress, to find an approach to disarmament which would be so far-reaching yet realistic, so mutually balanced and beneficial, that it could be accepted by every nation. And it is in this spirit that we have presented with the agreement of the Soviet Union under the label both nations now accept of "general and complete disarmament"—a new statement of newly-agreed principles for negotiation.

But we are well aware that all issues of principle are not settled, and that principles alone are not enough. It is therefore our intention to challenge the Soviet Union, not to an arms race, but to a peace race—to advance together step by step, stage by stage, until general and complete disarmament has been achieved. We invite them now to go beyond agreement in principle to reach agreement on actual plans.

The program to be presented to this assembly—for general and complete Disarmament under effective international control—moves to bridge the gap between those who insist on a gradual approach and those who talk only of the final and total achievement. It would create machinery to keep the peace as it destroys the machinery of war. It would proceed through balanced and safeguarded stages designed to give no state a military advantage over another. It would place the final responsibility for verification and control where it belongs, not with the big powers alone, not with one's adversary or one's self, but in an international organization within the framework of the United Nations. It would assure that indispensable condition of disarmament—true inspection—and apply it in stages proportionate to the stage of disarmament. It would cover delivery systems as well as weapons. It would ultimately halt their production as well as their testing, their transfer as well as their possession. It would achieve, under the eyes of an international disarmament organization, a steady reduction in force, both nuclear and conventional, until it has abolished all armies and all weapons except those needed for internal order and a new United Nations Peace Force. And it starts that process now, today, even as the talks begin.

In short, general and complete disarmament must no longer be a slogan, used to resist the first steps. It is no longer to be a goal without means of achieving it, without means of verifying its progress, without means of keeping the peace. It is now a realistic plan, and a test—a test of those only willing to talk and a test of those willing to act.

Such a plan would not bring a world free from conflict and greed—but it the era of the super state—but it would usher in an era in which no state could annihilate or be annihilated by another.

In 1945, this Nation proposed the Baruch Plan to internationalize the atom before other nations even possessed the bomb or demilitarized their troops. We proposed with our allies the Disarmament Plan of 1951 while still at war in Korea. And we make our proposals today, while building up our defenses over Berlin, not because we are inconsistent or insincere or intimidated, but because we know the rights of free men will prevail-because while we are compelled against our will to rearm, we look confidently beyond Berlin to the kind of disarmed world we all prefer.

I therefore propose, on the basis of this Plan, that disarmament negotiations resume promptly, and continue without interruption until an entire program for general and complete disarmament has not only been agreed but has been actually achieved.

The logical place to begin is a treaty assuring the end of nuclear tests of all kinds, in every environment, under workable controls. The United States and the United Kingdom have proposed such a treaty that is both reasonable, effective and ready for signature. We are still prepared to sign that treaty today.

We also proposed a mutual ban on atmospheric testing, without inspection or controls, in order to save the human race from the poison of radioactive fallout. We regret that offer has not been accepted.

For fifteen years we have sought to make the atom an instrument of peaceful growth rather than of war. But for fifteen years our concessions have been matched by obstruction, our patience by intransigence. And the pleas of mankind for peace have met with disregard.

Finally, as the explosions of others beclouded the skies, my country was left with no alternative but to act in the interests of its own and the free world's security. We cannot endanger that security be refraining from testing while others improve their arsenals. Nor can we endanger it by another long, uninspected ban on testing. For three years we accepted those risks in cur open society while seeking agreement on inspection. But this year, while we were negotiating in good faith in Geneva, others were secretly preparing new experiments in destruction.

Our tests are not polluting the atmosphere. Our deterrent weapons are guarded against accidental explosion or use. Our doctors and scientists stand ready to help any nation measure and meet the hazards to health which inevitably result from the tests in the atmosphere.

But to halt the spread of these terrible weapons, to halt the contamination of the air, to halt the spiraling nuclear arms race, we remain ready to seek new avenues of agreement; our new Disarmament Program thus includes the following proposals.

-First, signing the test-ban treaty by all nations. This can be done now. Test ban negotiations need not and should not await general disarmament.

-Second, stopping the production of fissionable materials for use in weapons, and preventing their transfer to any nation now lacking in nuclear weapons.

-Third, prohibiting the transfer of control over nuclear weapons to states that do not own them.

-Fourth, keeping nuclear weapons from seeding new battlegrounds in outer space.

-Fifth, gradually destroying existing nuclear weapons and converting the materials to peaceful uses; and

-Finally, halting the unlimited testing and production of strategic nuclear delivery vehicles, and gradually destroying them as well.

To destroy arms, however, is not enough. We must create even as we destroy—creating worldwide law and law enforcement as we outlaw worldwide war and weapons. In the world we seek, the United Nations Emergency Forces which have been hastily assembled, uncertainly supplied, and inadequately financed, will never be enough.

Therefore, the United States recommends that all member nations earmark special peace-keeping units in their armed forces to be on call of the United Nations, to be specially trained and quickly available, and with advance provision for financial and logistic support.

In addition, the American delegation will suggest a series of steps to improve the United Nations' machinery for the peaceful settlement of disputes—for on-the-spot fact-finding, mediation and adjudication—for extending the rule of international law. For peace is not solely a matter of military or technical problems—it is primarily a problem of politics and people. And unless man can match his strides in weaponry and technology with equal strides in social and political development, our great strength, like that of the dinosaur, will become incapable of proper control—and like the dinosaur vanish from the earth.

As we extend the rule of law on earth, so must we also extend it to man's new domain—outer space.

All of us salute the brave cosmonauts of the Soviet Union. The new horizons of outer space must not be driven by the old concepts of imperialism and sovereign claims. The cold reaches of the universe must not become the new arena of an even colder war.

To this end, we shall urge proposals extending the United Nations Charter to the limits of man's exploration in the universe, reserving outer space for peaceful use, prohibiting weapons of mass destruction in space or on celestial bodies, and opening the mysteries and benefits of space to every nation.

We shall propose further cooperative efforts between all nations in weather prediction and eventually in weather control. We shall propose, finally, a global system of communications satellites linking the whole world in telegraph and telephone and radio and television. The day need not be far away when such a system will televise the proceedings of this body to every corner of the world for the benefit of peace.

But the mysteries of outer space must not divert our eyes or our energies the harsh realities that face our fellow men. Political sovereignty is but a mockery without the means of meeting poverty and illiteracy and disease. Self-determination is but a slogan if the future holds no hope.

This is why my Nation, which has freely shared its capital and its technology to help others help themselves, now proposes officially designating this decade of the 1960's as the United Nations Decade of Development. Under the framework of that Resolution, the United Nations' existing efforts in promoting economic growth can be expanded and coordinated. Regional surveys and training institutes can now pool the talents of many. New research, technical assistance and pilot projects can unlock the wealth of less developed lands and untapped waters. And development can become a cooperative and not a competitive enterprise - to enable all nations, however diverse in their systems and beliefs, to become in fact as well as in law free and equal nations.

My Country favors a world of free and equal states. We agree with those who say that colonialism is a key issue in this Assembly. But let the full facts of that issue be discussed in full. On the one hand is the fact that, since the close of World War II, a worldwide declaration of independence has transformed nearly 1 billion people and 9 million square miles into 42 free and independent states. Less than 2 percent of the world's population now lives in "dependent" territories.

I do not ignore the remaining problems of traditional colonialism which still confront this body. Those problems will be solved, with patience, good will, and determination. Within the limits of our responsibility in such matters, my Country intends to be a participant and not merely an observer, in the peaceful, expeditious movement of nations from the status of colonies to the partnership of equals. That continuing tide of self-determination, which runs so strong, has our sympathy and our support.

But colonialism in its harshest forms is not only the exploitation of new nations by old, of dark skins by light, or the subjugation of the poor by the rich. My Nation was once a colony, and we know what colonialism means; the exploitation and subjugation of the weak by the powerful, of the many by the few, of the governed who have given no consent to be governed, whatever their continent, their class, or their color. And that is why there is no ignoring the fact that the tide of self-determination has not reached the Communist empire where a population far larger than that officially termed "dependent" lives under governments installed by foreign troops instead of free institutions—under a system which knows only one party and one belief—which suppresses free debate, and free elections, and free newspapers, and free books and free trade unions—and which builds a wall to keep truth a stranger and its own citizens prisoners. Let us debate colonialism in full—and apply the principle of free choice and the practice of free plebiscites in every corner of the globe.

Finally, as President of the United States, I consider it my duty to report to this Assembly on two threats to the peace which are not on your crowded agenda, but which causes us, and most of you, the deepest concern.

The first threat on which I wish to report is widely misunderstood: the smoldering coals of war in Southeast Asia. South Viet-Nam is already under attack—sometimes by a single assassin, sometimes by a band of guerrillas, recently by full battalions. The peaceful borders of Burma, Cambodia, and India have been repeatedly violated. And the peaceful people of Laos are in danger of losing the independence they gained not so long ago.

No one can call these "wars of liberation." For these are free countries living under their own governments. Nor are these aggressions any less real because men are knifed in their homes and not shot in the fields of battle.

The very simple question confronting the world community is whether measures can be devised to protect the small and the weak from such tactics. For if they are successful in Laos and South Viet-Nam, the gates will be opened wide.

The United States seeks for itself no base, no territory, no special position in this area of any kind. We support a truly neutral and independent Laos, its people free from outside interference, living at peace with themselves and with their neighbors, assured that their territory will not be used for attacks on others, and under a government comparable (as Mr. Khrushchev and I agreed at Vienna) to Cambodia and Burma.

But now the negotiations over Laos are reaching a crucial stage, The cease-fire is at best precarious. The rainy season is coming to an end. Laotian territory is being used to infiltrate South Viet-Nam

The world community must recognize—and all those who are involved—that this potent threat to Laotian peace and freedom is indivisible from all other threats to their own

Secondly, I wish to report to you on the crisis over Germany and Berlin. This is not the time or the place for immoderate tones, but the world community is entitled to know the very simple issues as we see them.

If there is a crisis it is because an existing peace is under threat, because an existing island of free people is under pressure, because solemn agreements are being treated with indifference. Established international rights are being threatened with unilateral usurpation. Peaceful circulation has been interrupted by barbed wire and concrete blocks.

One recalls the order of the Czar in Pushkin's Boris Godunov: "Take steps at this very hour that our frontiers be fenced in by barriers ... That not a single soul pass o'er the border, that not a hare be able to run or a crow to fly."

It is absurd to allege that we are threatening a war merely to prevent the Soviet Union and East Germany from signing a so-called "treaty" of peace. The Western Allies are not concerned with any paper arrangements the Soviets may wish to make with a regime of their own creation, on territory occupied by their own troops and governed by their own agents. No such action can affect either our rights or our responsibilities.

If there is a dangerous crisis in Berlin—and there is—it is because of threats against the vital interests and the deep commitments of the

Western Powers, and the freedom of West Berlin. We cannot yield these interests. We cannot fail these commitments. We cannot surrender the freedom of these people for whom we are responsible. A "peace treaty" which carried with it the provisions which destroy the peace would be a fraud. A "free city" which was not genuinely free would suffocate freedom and would be an infamy.

For a city or a people to be truly free, they must have the secure right, without economic, political or police pressure, to make their own choice and to live their own lives. And as I have said before, if anyone doubts the extent to which our presence is desired by the people of West Berlin, we are ready to have that question submitted to a free vote in all Berlin, and if possible, among all the German people.

The elementary fact about this crisis is that it is unnecessary. The elementary tools for a peaceful settlement are to be found in the charter. Under its law, agreements are to be kept, unless changed by all those who made them. Established rights are to be respected. The political disposition of peoples should rest upon their own wishes, freely expressed in plebiscites or free elections. If there are legal problems, they can be solved by legal means. If there is a threat of force, it must be rejected. If there is desire for change, it must be a subject for negotiation and if there is negotiation, it must be rooted in mutual respect and concern for the rights of others.

The Western Powers have calmly resolved to defend, by whatever means are forced upon them, their obligations and their access to the free citizens of West Berlin and the self-determination of those citizens. This generation learned from bitter experience that either brandishing or yielding to threats can only lead to war. But firmness and reason can lead to the kind of peaceful solution in which my country profoundly believes.

We are committed to no rigid formula. We see no perfect solution. We recognize that troops and tanks can, for a time, keep a nation divided against its will, however unwise that policy may seem to us. But we believe a peaceful agreement is possible which protects the freedom of West Berlin and allied presence and access, while recognizing the historic and legitimate interests of others in assuring European security.

The possibilities of negotiation are now being explored; it is too early to report what the prospects may be. For our part, we would be glad to report at the appropriate time that a solution has been found. For there is no need for a crisis over Berlin, threatening the peace—and if those who created this crisis desire peace, there will be peace and freedom in Berlin.

The events and decisions of the next ten months may well decide the fate of man for the next ten thousand years. There will be no avoiding those events. There will be no appeal from these decisions. And we in this hall shall be remembered either as part of the generation that turned this planet into a flaming funeral pyre or the generation that met its vow "to save succeeding generations from the scourge of war."

In the endeavor to meet that vow, I pledge you every effort this Nation possesses. I pledge you that we shall neither commit nor provoke aggression, that we shall neither flee nor invoke the threat of force, that we shall never negotiate out of fear, but we shall never fear to negotiate.

Terror is not a new weapon. Throughout history it has been used by those who could not prevail, either by persuasion or example. But inevitably they fail, either because men are not afraid to die for a life worth living, or because the terrorists themselves came to realize that free men cannot be frightened by threats, and that aggression would meet its own response. And it is in the light of that history that every nation today should know, be he friend or foe, that the United States has both the will and the weapons to join free men in standing up to their responsibilities.

But I come here today to look across this world of threats to a world of peace. In that search we cannot expect any final triumph—for new problems will always arise. We cannot expect that all nations will adopt like systems—for conformity is the jailor of freedom, and the enemy of growth. Nor can we expect to reach our goal by contrivance, by fiat or even by the wishes of all.

But however close we sometimes seem to that dark and final abyss, let no man of peace and freedom despair. For he does not stand alone. If we all can persevere, if we can in every land and office look beyond our own shores and ambitions, then surely the age will dawn in which the strong are just and the weak secure and the peace preserved.

Ladies and gentlemen of this Assembly, the decision is ours. Never have the nations of the world had so much to lose, or so much to gain. Together we shall save our planet, or together we shall perish in its flames. Save it we can—and save it we must—and then shall we earn the eternal thanks of mankind and, as peacemakers, the eternal blessing of God.

Document VI

President John F Kennedy

ESTABLISHING THE U.S. ARMS CONTROL AND DISARMAMENT AGENCY*

Remarks Upon Signing the Bill

September 26, 1961

WITH THE SIGNING of H.R. 9118, there is created the United States Arms Control and Disarmament Agency. This act symbolizes the importance the United States places on arms control and disarmament in its foreign policy.

The creation for the first time by act of Congress of a special organization to deal with arms control and disarmament matters emphasizes the high priority that attaches to our efforts in this direction.

Our ultimate goal, as the act points out, is a world free from war and free from the dangers and burdens of armaments in which the use of force is subordinated to the rule of law and in which international adjustments to a changing world are achieved peacefully. It is a complex and difficult task to reconcile through negotiation the many security interests of all nations to achieve disarmament, but the establishment of this agency will provide new and better tools for this effort.

I am pleased and heartened by the bipartisan support this bill enjoyed in the Congress. The leaders of both political parties gave encouragement and assistance. The new agency brings renewed hope for agreement and progress in the critical battle for the survival of mankind.

---

*Public Papers of the Presidents of the United States: John F. Kennedy. Containing the Messages, Speeches and Statements of the President, January 20 to December 31, 1961 (Washington, DC: US Government Printing Office 1962), 626-27.

Document VII

President John F. Kennedy

Excerpt from

THE SECOND STATE OF THE UNION MESSAGE*

January 11, 1962

But arms alone are not enough to keep the peace; it must be kept by men. Our instrument and our hope is the United Nations, and I see little merit in the impatience of those who would abandon this imperfect world instrument because they dislike our imperfect world. For the troubles of a world organization merely reflect the troubles of the world itself. And if the organization is weakened, these troubles can only increase. We may not always agree with every detailed action taken by every officer of the United Nations, or with every voting majority. But as an institution, it should have in the future, as it has had in the past since its inception, no stronger or more faithful member than the United States of America.

In 1961 the peace-keeping strength of the United Nations was reinforced. And those who preferred or predicted its demise, envisioning a troika in the seat of Hammarskjold, or Red China inside the Assembly, have seen instead a new vigor, under a new Secretary General and a fully independent Secretariat. In making plans for a new forum and principles on disarmament, for peace-keeping in outer space, for a decade of development effort, the U.N. fulfilled its Charter's lofty aim.

Eighteen months ago the tangled, turbulent Congo presented the U.N. with its gravest challenge. The prospect was one of chaos, or certain big-power confrontation, with all of its hazards and all of its risks, to us and to others. Today the hopes have improved for peaceful conciliation within a united Congo. This is the objective of our policy in this important area.

No policeman is universally popular, particularly when he uses his stick to restore law and order on his beat. Those members who are willing to contribute their votes and their views, but very little else, have created a serious deficit by refusing to pay their share of special U.N. assessments. Yet they do pay their annual assessments to retain their votes, and a new U.N. bond issue, financing special operations for the next eighteen months, is to be repaid with interest from these regular assessments. This is clearly in our interest. It will not only keep the U.N. solvent, but require all voting members to pay their fair share of its activities. Our share of special operations has long been much higher than our share of the annual assessment, and the bond issue will in effect reduce our disproportionate obligation, and for these reasons I am urging Congress to approve our participation.

Public Papers of the Presidents of the United States: John F. Kennedy, Containing the Messages, Speeches and Statements of the President. January 1 to December 31, 1962 (Washington, DC: US Government Printing Office, 1963), 213-14.

Document VIII

President John F. Kennedy

Message to

THE AMERICAN ASSOCIATION FOR THE UNITED NATIONS *

March 12, 1962

The Twelfth Annual Conference of National Organizations called by the American Association for the United Nations comes as a propitious reminder of the range and depth of this country's support of the United Nations.

Both by its promise and by its actions, the U.N. has justified that support over the years.

The Sixteenth Session of the General Assembly ended last month with a matchless record of solid accomplishments.

It rejected emphatically a powerful attack against the integrity of the Secretariat and went on to a series of positive steps which are admirably summarized in the theme of your conference "The U.N. Decade of Development."

In the course of its work the Sixteenth General Assembly adopted a set of guiding principles and agreed to the new approach to general and complete disarmament which will get under way in Geneva on Wednesday. It extended the Charter of the United Nations to outer space and established a new Committee on the Peaceful Uses of Outer Space which begins its work next week. It adopted a resolution calling for an expanded and intensified program for economic and social progress in the less developed world in the decade ahead.

We can be proud of our initiatives and of the U.N. response in these three critical areas of disarmament, outer space, and rapid modernization of

---

*Public Papers of the Presidents of the United States: John F. Kennedy. Containing the Messages, Speeches and Statements of the President, January 1 to December 31, 1962 (Washington, DC: US Government Printing Office, 1963), 213-14.

the emerging nations. If real progress can be made in these three areas, the present decade can be the most exciting and rewarding time in history.

To sustain its present initiative as a force for peace and human progress the U.N., of course, must regain a sound and orderly financial position. The three-point financial plan approved by the General Assembly is the only proposal put forth at the U.N. or elsewhere which will meet the requirements and is the only one which has the approval of the General Assembly. The U. N. bond issue, which is the key part of the financing plan, has become the symbol and substance of support of the United Nations by its members.

Last week Finland and Norway purchased the first of the U.N. bonds. A dozen more nations will follow shortly. The world is now watching to see whether the United States will continue to play its full part in helping the United Nations to make this a decade in which the world moves dramatically toward the peaceful and progressive world foreseen in the Charter.

I look forward to meeting with your leaders at the 'White House tomorrow, and I welcome the evidence offered by your organizations that bipartisan support for the U.N. in its present financial crisis is stronger than ever. Please accept my best wishes for a most productive conference.

Document IX

President John F. Kennedy

Excerpt from

THE THIRD STATE OF THE UNION MESSAGE *

January 14, 1963

Finally, what can we do to move from the present pause toward enduring peace? Again I would counsel caution. I foresee no spectacular reversal in Communist methods or goals. But if all these trends and developments can persuade the Soviet Union to walk the path of peace, then let her know that all free nations will join with her. But until that choice is made; and until the world can develop a reliable system of international security, the free peoples have no choice but to keep their arms near.

This country, therefore, continues to require the best defense in the world—a defense which is suited to the sixties. This means, unfortunately, a rising defense budget—for there is no substitute for adequate defense, and no "bargain basement" way of achieving it. It means the expenditure of more than $15 billion this year on nuclear weapons systems alone, a sum which is about equal to the combined defense budgets of our European Allies.

But it also means improved air and missile defenses, improved civil defense, a strengthened anti-guerrilla capacity and flexible non-nuclear forces. For threats of massive retaliation may not deter piecemeal aggression—and a line of destroyers in a quarantine, or a division of well-equipped men on a border, may be more useful to our real security than the multiplication of awesome weapons beyond all rational need.

But our commitment to national safety is not a commitment to expand our Military Establishment indefinitely. We do not dismiss disarmament as an idle dream. For we believe that, in the end, it is the only way of assuring the security of all without impairing the interests of any. Nor do we mistake honorable negotiation for appeasement. While we shall never

*Public Papers of the Presidents of the United States: John F. Kennedy. Containing the Messages, Speeches and Statements of the President, January 1 to November 22, 1963 (Washington, DC: US Government Printing Office, 1964), 18-19.

weary in the defense of freedom, neither shall we abandon the pursuit of peace.

In this quest, the United Nations requires our full and continued support. Its value in serving the cause of peace has been shown anew in its role in the West New Guinea settlement, in its use as a forum for the::Cuban crisis, and in its task of unification in the Congo. Today the United Nations is primarily the protector of the small and the weak, and a safety valve for the strong. Tomorrow it can form the framework for a world of law—a world in which no nation dictates the destiny of another, and in which the vast resources now devoted to destructive means will serve constructive ends.

In short, let our adversaries choose. If they choose peaceful competition, they shall have it. If they come to realize that their ambitions cannot succeed—if they see that their "wars of liberation" and subversion will ultimately fail—if they recognize that there is more security in accepting inspection than in permitting new nations to master the black arts of nuclear weapons and war—and if they are willing to turn their energies, as we are, to the great unfinished tasks of our own peoples—then, surely, the areas of agreement can be very wide indeed: a clear understanding about Berlin, stability in southeast Asia, an end to nuclear testing, new checks on surprise or accidental attack, and, ultimately, general and complete disarmament.

Document X

President John F. Kennedy

DISARMAMENT IS OUR GOAL*

Address Delivered at Commencement
American University at Washington, D.C.

June 10, 1963

Professor Woodrow Wilson once said that every man sent out from a university should be a man of his nation as well as a man of his time and I'm confident that the men and women who carry the honor of graduating from this institution will continue to give from their lives, from their talents a high measure of public service and public support.

"There are few earthly things more beautiful than a University," wrote John Masefield, in his tribute to the English universities, and his words are equally true here. He did not refer to spires and towers, to campus greens and ivied walls. He admired the splendid beauty of the university, he said, because it was "a place where those who hate ignorance may strive to know, where those who perceive truth may strive to make others see."

I have therefore chosen this time and this place to discuss a topic on which ignorance too often abounds and the truth is too rarely perceived, yet it is the most important topic on earth: world peace.

What kind of a peace do I mean? What kind of peace do we seek? Not a Pax Americana enforced on the world by American weapons of war. Not the peace of the grave or the security of the slave. I am talking about genuine peace, the kind of peace that makes life on earth worth living, the kind that enables men and nations to grow and to hope and to build a better life for their children—not merely peace for Americans, but peace for all men and women; not merely peace in our time, but peace for all time.

---

*Public Papers of the Presidents of the United States: John F. Kennedy. Containing the Messages, Speeches and Statements of the President, January 1 to November 22, 1963 (Washington, DC: US Government Printing Office, 1964), 459-64.

I speak of peace because of the new face of war. Total war makes no sense in an age when great powers can maintain large and relatively invulnerable nuclear forces and refuse to surrender without resort to forces. It makes no sense in an age when a single nuclear weapon contains almost ten times the explosive force delivered by all of the Allied air forces in the Second World War. It makes no sense in an age when the deadly poisons produced by a nuclear exchange would be carried by the wind and water and soil and seed to the far corners of the globe and to generations yet unborn.

Today the expenditure of billions of dollars every year on weapons acquired for the purpose of making sure we never need to use them is essential to keeping the peace. But surely the acquisition of such idle stockpiles, which can only destroy and never create, is not the only, much less the most efficient, means of assuring peace.

I speak of peace, therefore, as the necessary rational end of rational men. I realize that the pursuit of peace is not as dramatic as the pursuit of war, and frequently the words of the pursuer fall on deaf ears. But we have no more urgent task.

Some say that it is useless to speak of world peace or world law or world disarmament, and that it will be useless until the leaders of the Soviet Union adopt a more enlightened attitude. I hope they do. I believe we can help them do it. But I also believe that we must re-examine our attitude, as individuals and as a nation, for our attitude is as essential as theirs. And every graduate of this school, every thoughtful citizen who despairs of war and wishes to bring peace, should begin by looking inward, by examining his own attitude toward the possibilities of peace, toward the Soviet Union, toward the course of the Cold War, and toward freedom and peace here at home.

First, let us examine our attitude toward peace itself. Too many of us think it is impossible. Too many think it unreal. But that is a dangerous, defeatist belief. It leads to the conclusion that war is inevitable, that mankind is doomed, that we are gripped by forces we cannot control.

We need not accept that view. Our problems are man-made; therefore they can be solved by man. And man can be as big as he wants. No problem of human destiny is beyond human beings. Man's reason and spirit have often solved the seemingly unsolvable, and we believe they can do it again.

I am not referring to the absolute, infinite concept of universal peace and goodwill of which some fantasts and fanatics dream. I do not deny the value of hopes and dreams, but we merely invite discouragement and incredulity by making them our only and immediate goal.

Let us focus instead on a more practical, more attainable peace, based not on a sudden revolution in human nature but on a gradual evolution in human institutions, on a series of concrete actions and effective agreements which are in the interest of all concerned. There is no single, simple key to this peace, no grand or magic formula to be adopted by one or two powers. Genuine peace must be the product of many nations, the sum of many acts. It must be dynamic, not static, changing to meet the challenge of each new generation. For peace is a process, a way of solving problems.

With such a peace there will still be quarrels and conflicting interests, as there are within families and nations. World peace, like community peace, does not require that each man love his neighbor; it requires only that they live together in mutual tolerance, submitting their disputes to a just and peaceful settlement. And history teaches us that enmities between nations, as between individuals, do not last forever. However fixed our likes and dislikes may seem, the tide of time and events will often bring surprising changes in the relations between nations and neighbors.

So let us persevere. Peace need not be impracticable, and war need not be inevitable. By defining our goal more clearly, by making it seem more manageable and less remote, we can help all peoples to see it, to draw hope from it, and to move irresistibly toward it.

Second, let us re-examine our attitude toward the Soviet Union. It is discouraging to think that their leaders may actually believe what their propagandists write. It is discouraging to read a recent authoritative Soviet text on military strategy and find, on page after page, wholly baseless and incredible claims—such as the allegation that "American imperialist circles are preparing to unleash different types of wars ... that there is a very real threat of a preventive war being unleashed by American imperialists against the Soviet Union ... [and that] the political aims of the American imperialists are to enslave economically and politically the European and other capitalist countries ... [and] to achieve world domination ... by means of aggressive wars."

Truly as it was written long ago: "The wicked flee when no man pursueth."

Yet it is sad to read these Soviet statements, to realize the extent of the gulf between us. But it is also a warning—a warning to the American people not to fall into the same trap as the Soviets, not to see only a distorted and desperate view of the other side, not to see conflict as inevitable, accommodation .as impossible, and communication as nothing more than an exchange of threats.

No government or social system is so evil that its people must be considered as lacking in virtue. As Americans we find Communism profoundly repugnant as a negation of personal freedom and dignity. But we can still hail the Russian people for their many achievements—in science and space, in economic and industrial growth, in culture and in acts of courage.

Among the many traits the peoples of our two countries have in common, none is stronger than our mutual abhorrence of war. Almost unique among the major world powers, we have never been at war with each other. And no nation in the history of battle ever suffered more than the Soviet Union suffered in the course of the Second World War. At least twenty million lost their lives. Countless millions of homes and farms were burned or sacked. A third of the nation's territory, including nearly two-thirds its industrial base, was turned into a wasteland—a loss equivalent to the devastation of this country east of Chicago.

Today, should total war ever break out again, no matter how, our two countries would become the primary targets. It is an ironical but accurate fact that the two strongest powers are the two in the most danger of devastation. All we have built, all we have worked for, would be destroyed in the first twenty-four hours. And even in the Cold War, which brings burdens and dangers to so many countries, including this nation's closest allies, our two countries bear the heaviest burdens. For we are both devoting massive sums of money to weapons that could be better devoted to combating ignorance, poverty and disease. We are both caught up in a vicious and dangerous cycle in which suspicion on one side breeds suspicion on the other and new weapons beget counter weapons.

In short, both the United States and its allies, and the Soviet Union and its allies, have a mutually deep interest in a just and genuine peace and in halting the arms race. Agreements to this end are in the interests of the

Soviet Union as well as ours, and even the most hostile nations can be relied upon to accept and keep those treaty obligations, and only those treaty obligations, which are in their own interest.

So let us not be blind to our differences, but let us also direct attention to our common interests and to the means by which those differences can be resolved. And if we cannot end now our differences, at least we can help make the world safe for diversity. For in the final analysis our most basic common link is that we all inhabit this planet. We all breathe the same air. We all cherish our children's future. And we are all mortal.

Third, let us re-examine our attitude toward the Cold War, remembering that we are not engaged in a debate, seeking to pile up debating points. We are not here distributing blame or pointing the finger of judgment. We must deal with the world as it is and not as it might have been had the history of the last eighteen years been different.

We must, therefore, persevere in search for peace in the hope that constructive changes with the Communist bloc might bring within reach solutions which now seem beyond us. We must conduct our affairs in such a way that it becomes in the Communists' interest to agree on a genuine peace. Above all, while defending our own vital interests, nuclear powers must avert those confrontations which bring an adversary to a choice of either a humiliating retreat or a nuclear war. To adopt that kind of course in the nuclear age would be evidence only of the bankruptcy of our policy or of a collective death wish for the world.

To secure these ends, America's weapons are non-provocative— carefully controlled, designed to deter and capable of selective use. Our military forces are committed to peace and disciplined in self-restraint. Our diplomats are instructed to avoid unnecessary irritants and purely rhetorical hostility.

For we can seek a relaxation of tensions without relaxing our guard. And, for our part, we do not need to use threats to prove that we are resolute. We do not need to jam foreign broadcasts out of fear our faith will be eroded. We are unwilling to impose our system on any unwilling people, but we are willing and able to engage in peaceful competition with any people on earth.

Meanwhile we seek to strengthen the United Nations, to help solve its financial problems, to make it a more effective instrument of peace, to develop it into a genuine world security system—a system capable of resolving disputes on the basis of law, of insuring the security of the large and the small, and of creating conditions under which arms can finally be abolished.

Document XI

President John F. Kennedy

A TEST BAN TREATY IS ANNOUNCED*

A Television Address to the People

July 26, 1963

I speak to you tonight in a spirit of hope. Eighteen years ago the advent of nuclear weapons changed the course of the world as well as the war. Since that time, all mankind has been struggling to escape from the darkening prospect of mass destruction on earth. In an age when both sides have come to possess enough nuclear power to destroy the human race several times over, the world of Communism and the world of free choice have been caught up in a vicious circle of conflicting ideology and interest. Each increase of tension has produced an increase of arms; each increase of arms has produced an increase of tension.

In these years the United States and the Soviet Union have frequently communicated suspicion and warnings to each other, but very rarely hope. Our representatives have met at the summit and at the brink; they have met in Washington and in Moscow, in Geneva and at the United Nations. But too often these meetings have produced only darkness, discord or disillusion.

Yesterday a shaft of light cut into the darkness. Negotiations were concluded in Moscow on a treaty to ban all nuclear tests in the atmosphere, in outer space and underwater. For the first time, an agreement has been reached on bringing the forces of nuclear destruction under international control-a goal first sought in 1946 when Bernard Baruch presented a comprehensive control plan to the United Nations.

That plan and many subsequent disarmament plans, large and small, have all been blocked by those opposed to international inspection. A ban on nuclear tests, however, requires on-the-spot inspection only for underground tests. This Nation now possesses a variety of techniques to

---

*Public Papers of the Presidents of the United States: John F. Kennedy. Containing the Messages, Speeches and Statements of the President. January 1 to November 22, 1963 (Washington, DC: US Government Printing Office, 1964), 601-06.

detect the nuclear tests of other nations which are conducted in the air or underwater. For such tests produce unmistakable signs which our modern instruments can pick up.

The treaty initialed yesterday, therefore, is a limited treaty which permits continued underground testing and prohibits only those tests that we ourselves can police. It requires no control posts, no on-site inspection no international body.

We should also understand that it has other limits as well. Any nation which signs the treaty will have an opportunity to withdraw if it finds that extraordinary events related to the subject matter of the treaty have jeopardized its supreme interests; and no nation's right of self-defense will in any way be impaired. Nor does this treaty mean an end to the threat of nuclear war. It will not reduce nuclear stockpiles; it will not halt the production of nuclear weapons; it will not restrict their use in time of war.

Nevertheless, this limited treaty will radically reduce the nuclear testing which would otherwise be conducted on both sides; it will prohibit the United States, the United Kingdom, the Soviet Union and all others who sign it from engaging in the atmospheric tests which have so alarmed mankind; and it offers to all the world a welcome sign of hope.

For this is not a unilateral moratorium, but a specific and solemn legal obligation. While it will not prevent this nation from testing underground, or from being ready to conduct atmospheric tests if the acts of others so require, it gives us a concrete opportunity to extend its coverage to other nations and later to other forms of nuclear tests.

This treaty is in part the product of Western patience and vigilance. We have made clear, most recently in Berlin and Cuba, our deep resolve to protect our security and our freedom against any form of aggression. We have also made clear our steadfast determination to limit the arms race. In three administrations our soldiers and diplomats have worked together to this end, always supported by Great Britain. Prime Minister Macmillan joined with President Eisenhower in proposing a limited test ban in 1959, and again with me in 1961 and 1962.

But the achievement of this goal is not a victory for one side; it is a victory for mankind. It reflects no concessions either to or by the Soviet Union. It reflects simply our common recognition of the dangers in further testing.

This treaty is not the millennium. It will not resolve all conflicts, or cause the Communists to forgo their ambitions, or eliminate the dangers of war. It will not reduce our need for arms or allies or programs of assistance to others. But it is an important first step—a step toward peace, a step toward reason, a step away from war.

Here is what this step can mean to you and to your children and your neighbors. First, this treaty can be a step toward reduced world tension and broader areas of agreement. The Moscow talks have reached no agreement on any other subject, nor is this treaty conditioned on any other matter. Under Secretary Harriman made it clear that any nonaggression arrangements across the division in Europe would require full consultation with our allies and full attention to their interests. He also made clear our strong preference for a more comprehensive treaty banning all tests everywhere and our ultimate hope for general and complete disarmament. The Soviet Government, however, is still unwilling to accept the inspection such goals require.

No one can predict with certainty, therefore, what further agreements, if any, can be built on the foundations of this one. They could include controls on preparations for surprise attack or on numbers and type of armaments, there could be further limitations on the spread of nuclear weapons. The important point is that efforts to seek new agreements will go forward.

But the difficulty of predicting the next step is no reason to be reluctant about this step. Nuclear test ban negotiations have long been a symbol of East-West disagreement. If this treaty can also be a symbol, if it can symbolize the end of one era and the beginning of another, if both sides can by this treaty gain confidence and experience in peaceful collaboration, then this short and simple treaty may well become an historic mark in man's age-old pursuit of peace.

Western policies have long been designed to persuade the Soviet Union to renounce aggression, direct or indirect, so that their people and all people may live and let live in peace. The unlimited testing of new weapons of war cannot lead toward that end, but this treaty, if it can be followed by further progress, can clearly move in that direction.

I do not say that a world without aggression or threats of war would be an easy world. It will bring new problems, new challenges from the

Communists, new dangers of relaxing our vigilance or of mistaking their intent.

But those dangers pale in comparison to those of the spiraling arms race and a collision course toward war. Since the beginning of history, war has been mankind's constant companion. It has been the rule, not the exception. Even a nation as young and as peace-loving as our own has fought through eight wars. And three times in the last two years and a half I have been required to report to you as President that this nation and the Soviet Union stood on the verge of direct military confrontation in Laos, in Berlin and in Cuba.

A war today or tomorrow, if it led to nuclear war, would not be like any war in history. A full-scale nuclear exchange, lasting less than sixty minutes, with the weapons now in existence, could wipe out more than 300 million Americans, Europeans and Russians, as well as untold numbers elsewhere. And the survivors, as Chairman Khrushchev warned the Communist Chinese, "The survivors would envy the dead. "For they would inherit a world so devastated by explosions and poison and fire that today we cannot even conceive of its horrors. So let us try to turn the world from war. Let us make the most of this opportunity, and every opportunity, to reduce tension, to slow down the perilous nuclear arms race and to check the world's slide toward final annihilation.

Second, this treaty can be a step toward freeing the world from the fears and dangers of radioactive fallout. Our own atmospheric tests last year were conducted under conditions which restricted such fallout to an absolute minimum. But over the years the number and the yield of weapons tested have rapidly increased and so have the radioactive hazards from such testing. Continued unrestricted testing by the nuclear powers, joined in time by other nations which may be less adept in limiting pollution, will increasingly contaminate the air that all of us must breathe.

Even then the number of children and grandchildren with cancer in their bones, with leukemia in their blood or with poison in their lungs might seem statistically small to some in comparison with natural health hazards. But this is not a natural health hazard, and it is not a statistical issue. The loss of even one human life or the malformation of even one baby, who may be born long after we are gone, should be of concern to us all. Our children and grandchildren are not merely statistics toward which we can be indifferent.

Nor does this affect the nuclear powers alone. These tests befoul the air of all men and all nations, the committed and the uncommitted alike, without their knowledge and without their consent. That is why the continuation of atmospheric testing causes so many countries to regard all nuclear powers as equally evil; and we can hope that its prevention will enable those countries to see the world more clearly, while enabling all the world to breathe more easily.

Third, this treaty can be a step toward preventing the spread of nuclear weapons to nations not now possessing them. During the next several years, in addition to the four current nuclear powers, a small but significant number of nations will have the intellectual, physical and financial resources to produce both nuclear weapons and the means of delivering them. In time, it is estimated, many other nations will have either this capacity or other ways of obtaining nuclear warheads, even as missiles can be commercially purchased today.

I ask you to stop and think for a moment what it would mean to have nuclear weapons in so many hands, in the hands of countries large and small, stable and unstable, responsible and irresponsible, scattered throughout the world. There would be no rest for anyone then, no stability, no real security and no chance of effective disarmament. There would only be the increased chance of accidental war and an increased necessity for the great powers to involve themselves in what otherwise would be local conflicts.

If only one thermonuclear bomb were to be dropped on any American, Russian or any other city, whether it was launched by accident or design, by a madman or by an enemy, by a large nation or by a small, from any corner of the world, that one bomb could release more destructive power on the inhabitants of that one helpless city than all the bombs dropped in the Second World War.

Neither the United States nor the Soviet Union nor the United Kingdom nor France can look forward to that day with equanimity. We have a great obligation—all four nuclear powers have a great obligation—to use whatever time remains to prevent the spread of nuclear weapons, to persuade other countries not to test, transfer, acquire, possess or produce such weapons.

This treaty can be the opening wedge in that campaign. It provides that none of the parties will assist other nations to test in the forbidden environments. It opens the door for further agreements on the control of nuclear weapons, and it is open for all nations to sign; for it is in the interest of all nations, and already we have heard from a number of countries who wish to join us promptly.

Fourth and finally, this treaty can limit the nuclear arms race in ways which, on balance, will strengthen our nation's security far more than the continuation of unrestricted testing. For in today's world a nation's security does not always increase as it arms increase when its adversary is doing the same, and unlimited competition in the testing and development of new types of destructive nuclear weapons will not make the world safer for either side. Under this limited treaty, on the other hand, the testing of other nations could never be sufficient to offset the ability of our strategic forces to deter or survive a nuclear attack and to penetrate and destroy an aggressor's homeland.

We have, and under this treaty we will continue to have, the nuclear strength that we need. It is true that the Soviets have tested nuclear weapons of a yield higher than that which we thought to be necessary, but the hundred-megaton bomb of which they spoke two years ago does not and will not change the balance of strategic power. The United States has chosen, deliberately, to concentrate on more mobile and more efficient weapons, with lower but entirely sufficient yield, and our security is, therefore, not impaired by the treaty I am discussing.

It is also true, as Mr. Khrushchev would agree that nations cannot afford in these matters to rely simply on the good faith of their adversaries. We have not, therefore, overlooked the risk of secret violations. There is at present a possibility that deep in outer space, hundreds of thousands of millions of miles away from the earth, illegal tests might go undetected. But we already have the capability to construct a system of observation that would make such tests almost impossible to conceal, and we can decide at any time whether such a system is needed in the light of the limited risk to us and the limited reward to others of violations attempted at that range. For any tests which might be conducted so far out in space which cannot be conducted more easily and efficiently and legally underground would necessarily be of such a magnitude that they would be extremely difficult to conceal. We can also employ new devices to check on the testing of smaller weapons in the lower atmosphere. Any violation, moreover, involves, along with the risk of detection, the end of the treaty and the world-wide consequences for the violator.

Secret violations are possible and secret preparations for a sudden withdrawal are possible and thus our own vigilance and strength must be maintained, as we remain ready to withdraw and to resume all forms of testing if we must. But it would be a mistake to assume that this treaty will be quickly broken. The gains of illegal testing are obviously slight compared to their cost and the hazard of discovery, and the nations which have initialed and will sign this treaty prefer it, in my judgment, to unrestricted testing as a matter of their own self-interest, for these nations, too, and all nations, have a stake in limiting the arms race, in holding the spread of nuclear weapons and in breathing air that is not radioactive. While it may be theoretically possible to demonstrate the risks inherent in any treaty—and such risks in this treaty are small—the far greater risks to our security are the risks of unrestricted testing, the risk of a nuclear arms race, the risk of new nuclear powers, nuclear pollution and nuclear war.

This limited test ban, in our most careful judgment, is safer by far for the United States than an unlimited nuclear arms race. For all these reasons, I am hopeful that this nation will promptly approve the limited test ban treaty. There will, of course, be debate in the country and in the Senate. The Constitution wisely requires the advice and consent of the Senate to all treaties, and that consultation has already begun. All this is as it should be. A document which may mark an historic and constructive opportunity for the world deserves an historic and constructive debate.

It is my hope that all of you will take part in that debate for this treaty is for all of us. It is particularly for our children and our grandchildren, and they have no lobby here in Washington. This debate will involve military, scientific and political experts, but it must not be left to them alone. The right and the responsibility are yours.

If we are to open new doorways to peace, if we are to seize this rare opportunity for progress, if we are to be as bold and farsighted in our control of weapons as we have been in their invention, then let us now show all the world on this side of the wall and the other that a strong America also stands for peace.

There is no cause for complacency. We have learned in times past that the spirit of one moment or place can be gone in the next. We have been disappointed more than once, and we have no illusions now that there are short cuts on the road to peace. At many points around the globe the Communists are continuing their efforts to exploit weakness and poverty. Their concentration of nuclear and conventional arms must still be deterred.

The familiar contest between choice and coercion, the familiar places of danger and conflict are still there in Cuba, in Southeast Asia, in Berlin and all around the globe, still requiring all the strength and the vigilance that we can muster. Nothing could more greatly damage our cause than if we and our allies were to believe that peace has already been achieved and that our strength and unity were no longer required.

But now, for the first time in many years, the path of peace may be open. No one can be certain what the future will bring. No one can say whether the time has come for an easing of the struggle. But history and our own conscience will judge us more harshly if we do not now make every effort to test our hopes by action, and this is the place to begin. According to the ancient Chinese proverb, "A journey of a thousand miles must begin with a single step."

My fellow Americans, let us take that first step. Let us, if we can, get back from the shadows of war and seek out the way of peace. And if that journey is one thousand miles, or even more, let history record that we, in this land, at this time, took the first step.

Document XII

President John F. Kennedy

THE NUCLEAR TEST BAN TREATY*

Remarks at the News Conference

September 12, 1963

Ladies and gentlemen, I want to stress again how important it is that the United States Senate approve the pending nuclear test ban treaty. It has already been signed by more than ninety governments, and it is clearer now than ever that this small step towards peace will have significant gains. And I want to commend to the American people the two distinguished and outstanding speeches made by Senator [Mike] Mansfield [D. Montana] and Senator [Everett M.] Dirksen [R. Illinois], the Majority and the Minority Leaders, who in the great tradition of American bipartisanship and national interest I think put the case most effectively.

The treaty will enable all of us who inhabit the earth, our children and children's children, to breathe easier, free from the fear of nuclear test fallout. It will curb the spread of nuclear weapons to other countries, thereby holding out hope for a more peaceful and stable world. It will slow down the nuclear arms race without impairing the adequacy of this Nation's arsenal or security, and it will offer a small but important foundation on which a world of law can be built.

The Senate hearings and debate have been intensive and valuable, but they have not raised an argument in opposition which was not thoroughly considered by our military, scientific, legal, and foreign policy leaders before the treaty was signed.

This Nation has sought to bring nuclear weapons under international control since 1946. This particular kind of treaty has been sought by us since 1959. If we are to give it now only grudging support, if this small clearly beneficial step cannot be approved by the widest possible margin

*Public Papers of the Presidents of the United States: John F. Kennedy. Containing the Messages, Speeches and Statements of the President .January 1 to November 22, 1963 (Washington, D C: US.Government Printing Office, 1964), 672.

in the Senate, then this Nation cannot offer much leadership or hope for the future.

But, if the American people and the American Senate can demonstrate that we are as determined to achieve a peace and a just peace as we are to defend our freedom, I think future generations will honor the action that we took.

Document XIII

President John F. Kennedy

"ONE WORLD, ONE HUMAN RACE WITH ONE COMMON DESTINY"

Address before the General Assembly of the United Nations

September 20, 1963

... We meet again in the quest for peace.

Twenty-four months ago, when I last had the honor of addressing this body, the shadow of fear lay darkly across the world. The freedom of West Berlin was in immediate peril. Agreement on a neutral Laos seemed remote. The mandate of the United Nations in the Congo was under fire. The financial outlook for this organization was in doubt. Dag Hammarskjold was dead. The doctrine of troika was being pressed in his place, and atmospheric nuclear tests had been resumed by the Soviet Union.

Those were anxious days for mankind, and some men wondered aloud whether this organization could survive. But the Sixteenth and Seventeenth General Assemblies achieved not only survival but progress. Rising to its responsibility, the United Nations helped reduce the tensions and helped to hold back the darkness.

Today the clouds have lifted a little so that new rays of hope can break through. The pressures on West Berlin appear to be temporarily eased. Political unity in the Congo has been largely restored. A neutral coalition in Laos, while still in difficulty, is at least in being. The integrity of the United Nations Secretariat has been reaffirmed. A United Nations Decade of Development is under way. And, for the first time in seventeen years of effort, a specific step has been taken to limit the nuclear arms race.

Public Papers of the Presidents of the United States: John F. Kennedy. Containing the Messages, Speeches and Statements of the President .January 1 to November 22, 1963 (Washington, DC: US Government Printing Office, 1964), 693-98.

I refer, of course, to the treaty to ban nuclear tests in the atmosphere, outer space and underwater, concluded by the Soviet Union, the United Kingdom and the United States, and already signed by nearly one hundred countries. It has been hailed by people the world over who are thankful to be free from the fears of nuclear fallout, and I am confident that on next Tuesday at ten-thirty o'clock in the morning it will receive the overwhelming endorsement of the Senate of the United States.

The world has not escaped from the darkness. The long shadows of conflict and crisis envelop us still. But we meet today in an atmosphere of rising hope and at a moment of comparative calm. My presence here today is not a sign of crisis, but of confidence. I am not here to report on a new threat to the peace or new signs of war. I have come to salute the United Nations and to show the support of the American people for your daily deliberations.

For the value of this body's work is not dependent on the existence of emergencies, nor can the winning of peace consist only of dramatic victories. Peace is a daily, a weekly, a monthly process, gradually changing opinions, slowly eroding old barriers, quietly building new structures. And however undramatic the pursuit of peace, that pursuit must go on.

Today we may have reached a pause in the Cold War, but that is not a lasting peace. A test ban treaty is a milestone, but it is not the millennium. We have not been released from our obligations; we have been given an opportunity. And if we fail to make the most of this moment and this momentum; if we convert our new-found hopes and understandings into new walls and weapons of hostility, if this pause in the Cold War merely leads to its renewal and not to its end, then the indictment of posterity will rightly point its finger at us all. But if we can stretch this pause into a period of cooperation, if both sides can now gain new confidence and experience in concrete collaborations for peace, if we can now be as bold and farsighted in the control of deadly weapons as we have been in their creation, then surely this first small step can be the start of a long and fruitful journey.

The task of building the peace lies with the leaders of every nation, large and small. For the great powers have no monopoly on conflict or ambition. The Cold War is not the only expression of tension in this world, and the nuclear race is not the only arms race. Even little wars are dangerous in a nuclear world. The long labor of peace is an undertaking for every nation, and in this effort none of us can remain unaligned.

To this goal none can be uncommitted.

The reduction of global tension must not be an excuse for the narrow pursuit of self-interest. If the Soviet Union and the United States, with all their global interests and clashing commitments of ideology, and with nuclear weapons still aimed at each other today, can find areas of common interest and agreement, then surely other nations can do the same—nations caught in regional conflicts, in racial issues or in the death throes of old colonialism. Chronic disputes which divert precious resources from the needs of the people or drain the energies of both sides serve the interests of no one, and the badge of responsibility in the modem world is a willingness to seek peaceful solutions.

It is never too early to try; and it is never too late to talk; and it is high time that many disputes on the agenda of this Assembly were taken off the debating schedule and placed on the negotiating table.

The fact remains that the United States, as a major nuclear power, does have a special responsibility in the world. It is, in fact, a threefold responsibility: a responsibility to our own citizens, a responsibility to the people of the whole world who are affected by our decisions, and to the next generation of humanity. We believe the Soviet Union also has these special responsibilities, and that those responsibilities require our two nations to concentrate less on our differences and more on the means of resolving them peacefully. For too long both of us have increased our military budgets, our nuclear stockpiles and our capacity to destroy all life—human, animal, vegetable—without any corresponding increase in our security.

Our conflicts, to be sure, are real. Our concepts of the world are different. No service is performed by failing to make clear our disagreements. A central difference is the belief of the American people in self-determination for all people.

We believe that the people of Germany and Berlin must be free to reunite their capital and their country.

We believe that the people of Cuba must be free to secure the fruits of the revolution that has been betrayed from within and exploited from without. In short, we believe that in all the world—in Eastern Europe as well as Western in Southern Africa as well as Northern, in old nations as well as new—people must be free to choose their own future, without discrimination or dictation, without coercion or subversion.

These are the basic differences between the Soviet Union and the United States, and they cannot be concealed. So long as they exist, they set limits to agreement, and they forbid the relaxation of our vigilance. Our defense around the world will be maintained for the protection of freedom, and our determination to safeguard that freedom will measure up to any threat or challenge.

But I would say to the leaders of the Soviet Union, and to their people, that if either of our countries is to be fully secure, we need a much better weapon than the H-bomb, a weapon better than ballistic missiles or nuclear submarines, and that better weapon is peaceful cooperation.

We have, in recent years, agreed on a limited test ban treaty, on an emergency communications link between our capitals, on a statement of principles for disarmament, on an increase in cultural exchange, on cooperation in outer space, on the peaceful exploration of the Antarctic, and on tempering last year's crisis over Cuba.

I believe, therefore, that the Soviet Union and the United States, together with their allies, can achieve further agreements which spring from our mutual interest in avoiding mutual destruction.

There can be no doubt about the agenda of further steps. We must continue to seek agreements on measures which prevent war by accident or miscalculation. We must continue to seek agreement on safeguards against surprise attack, including observation posts at key points. We must continue to seek agreement on further measures to curb the nuclear arms race, by controlling the transfer of nuclear weapons, converting fissionable materials to peaceful purposes and banning underground testing with adequate inspection and enforcement. We must continue to seek agreement on a freer flow of information and people from East to West and West to East.

We must continue to seek agreement encouraged by yesterday's affirmative response to this proposal by the Soviet Foreign Minister, on an arrangement to keep weapons of mass destruction out of outer space. Let us get our negotiators back to the negotiating table to work out a practicable arrangement to this end.

In these and other ways, let us move up the steep and difficult path toward comprehensive disarmament, securing mutual confidence through mutual verification and building the institutions of peace as we dismantle the engines of war. We must not let failure to agree on all points delay agreements where agreement is possible. And we must not put forward proposals for propaganda purposes.

Finally, in a field where the United States and the Soviet Union have a special capacity—in the field of space—there is room for new cooperation, for further joint efforts in the regulation and exploration of space. I include among these possibilities a joint expedition to the moon. Space offers no problems of sovereignty. By resolution of this Assembly, the members of the United Nations have forsworn any claim to territorial rights in outer space or on celestial bodies, and declared that international law and the United Nations Charter will apply. Why, therefore, should man's first flight to the moon be a matter of national competition? Why should the United States and the Soviet Union, in preparing for such expeditions, become involved in immense duplications of research, construction and expenditure? Surely we should explore whether the scientists and the astronauts of our two countries—indeed, of all the world—cannot work together in the conquest of space, sending someday in this decade to the moon not the representatives of a single nation but the representatives of all our countries.

All these and other new steps toward peaceful cooperation may be possible. Most of them will require on our part full consultation with our allies, for their interests are as much involved as our own, and we will not make an agreement at their expense. Most of them will require long and careful negotiation. And most of them will require a new approach to the Cold War—a desire not to "bury" one's adversary, but to compete in a host of peaceful arenas: in ideas, in production and ultimately in service to all mankind.

The contest will continue—the contest between those who see a monolithic world and those who believe in diversity—but it should be a contest in leadership and responsibility instead of destruction, a contest in achievement instead of intimidation. Speaking for the United States of America, I welcome such a contest. For we believe that truth is stronger than error, and that freedom is more enduring than coercion. And in the contest for a better life, all the world can be a winner.

The effort to improve the conditions of man, however, is not a task for a few. It is the task of all nations, acting alone, acting in groups, acting in the United Nations; for plague and pestilence, and plunder and pollution, the hazards of nature and the hunger of children are the foes of every nation. The earth, the sea and the air are the concern of every nation. And science, technology and education can be the ally of every nation.

Never before has man had such capacity to control his own environment—to end thirst and hunger, to conquer poverty and disease, to banish illiteracy and massive human misery. We have the power to make this the best generation of mankind in the history of the world or to make it the last.

The United States since the close of the war has sent over $100 billion worth of assistance to nations seeking economic viability. And two years ago this week we formed a Peace Corps to help interested nations meet the needs for trained manpower.

Other industrialized nations whose economies were rebuilt not so long ago with some help from us are now in turn recognizing their responsibility to the less developed nations.

The provision of development assistance by individual nations must go on. But the United Nations also must play a larger role in helping bring to all men the fruits of modern science and industry. A United Nations conference on this subject held earlier this year at Geneva opened new vistas for the developing countries. Next year a United Nations Conference on Trade will consider the needs of these nations for new markets. And more than four-fifths of the entire United Nations system can be found today mobilizing the weapons of science and technology for the United Nations' Decade of Development.

But more can be done.

A world center for health communications under the World Health Organization would warn of epidemics and the adverse effects of certain drugs, as well as transmit the results of new experiments and new discoveries.

Regional research centers could advance our common medical knowledge and train new scientists and doctors for new nations.

A global system of satellites could provide communication and weather information for all corners of the earth.

A worldwide program of conservation could protect the forest and wild game preserves now in danger of extinction for all time, improve the marine harvest of food from our oceans, and prevent the contamination of air and water by industrial as well as nuclear pollution.

And, finally, a worldwide program of farm productivity and food distribution, similar to our country's "Food for Peace" program, could now give every child the food he needs.

But man does not live by bread alone, and members of this organization are committed by the Charter to promote and respect human rights. Those rights are not respected when a Buddhist priest is driven from his pagoda, when a synagogue is shut down, when a Protestant church cannot open a mission, when a cardinal is forced into hiding or when a crowded church service is bombed. The United States of America is opposed to discrimination and persecution on grounds of race and religion anywhere in the world, including our own nation. We are working to right the wrongs of our own country.

Through legislation and administrative action, through moral and legal commitment, this government has launched a determined effort to rid our nation of discrimination which has existed too long—in education, in housing, in transportation, in employment, in the Civil Service, in recreation and in places of public accommodation. And therefore, in this or any other forum, we do not hesitate to condemn racial or religious injustice, whether committed or permitted by friend or foe.

I know that some of you have experienced discrimination in this country. But I ask you to believe me when I tell you that this is not the wish of most Americans, that we share your regret and resentment, and that we intend to end such practices for all time to come, not only for our visitors but for our own citizens as well.

I hope that not only our nation but all other multiracial societies will meet these standards of fairness and justice. We are opposed to apartheid and all forms of human oppression. We do not advocate the rights of black Africans in order to drive out white Africans. Our concern is the right of all men to equal protection under the law; and since human rights are indivisible, this body cannot stand aside when those rights are abused and neglected by any member state.

New efforts are needed if this Assembly's Declaration of Human Rights, now fifteen years old, is to have full meaning. And new means should be found for promoting the free expression and trade of ideas, through travel and communication, and through increased exchanges of people and books and broadcasts. For as the world renounces the competition of weapons, competition in ideas must flourish, and that competition must be as full and as fair as possible.

The United States delegation will be prepared to suggest to the United Nations initiatives in the pursuit of all the goals .For this is an organization for peace, and peace cannot come without work and progress.

The peace-keeping record of the United Nations has been a proud one, though its tasks are always formidable. We are fortunate to have the skills of our distinguished Secretary General and the brave efforts of those who have been serving the cause of peace in the Congo, in the Middle East, in Korea and Kashmir, in West New Guinea and Malaysia. But what the United Nations has done in the past is less important than the tasks for the future. We cannot take its peace-keeping machinery for granted. That machinery must be soundly financed, which it cannot be if some members are allowed to prevent it from meeting its obligations by failing to meet their own. The United Nations must be supported by all those who exercise their franchise here. And its operations must be backed to the end.

Too often a project is undertaken in the excitement of a crisis, and then it begins to lose its appeal as the problems drag on and the bills pile up. But we must have the steadfastness to see every enterprise through.

It is, for example, most important not to jeopardize the extraordinary United Nations gains in the Congo. The nation which sought this organization's help only three years ago has now asked the United Nations' presence to remain a little longer. I believe this Assembly should do what is necessary to preserve the gains already made and to protect the new nation in its struggle for progress. Let us complete what we have started, for as the Scriptures tell us, "No man who puts his hand to the plow and looks back is fit for the Kingdom of God."

I also hope that the recent initiative of several members in preparing stand-by peace forces for United Nations call will encourage similar commitments by others. This nation remains ready to provide logistic and other material support.

Policing, moreover, is not enough without provision for pacific settlement. We should increase the resort to special missions of fact-finding and conciliation, make greater use of the International Court of Justice and accelerate the work of the International Law Commission.

The United Nations cannot survive as a static organization. Its obligations are increasing as well as its size. Its charter must be changed as well as its customs. The authors of that charter did not intend that it be frozen in perpetuity. The science of weapons and war has made us all, far more than eighteen years ago in San Francisco, one world and one human race, with one common destiny. In such a world absolute sovereignty no longer assures us of absolute security. The conventions of peace must pull abreast and then ahead of the inventions of war, The United Nations, building on its successes and learning from its failures, must be developed into a genuine world security system.

But peace does not rest in charters and covenants alone. It lies in the hearts and minds of all people. And in this world no act, no pact, no treaty, no organization can hope to preserve it without the support of the wholehearted commitment of all people. So let us not rest all our hopes on parchment and on paper. Let us strive to build peace, a desire for peace, a willingness to work for peace, in the hearts and minds of all of our people. I believe that we can. I believe the problems of human destiny are not beyond the reach of human beings.

Two years ago I told this body that the United States had proposed, and was willing to sign, a limited test ban treaty. Today that treaty has been signed. It will not put an end to war. It will not remove basic conflicts. It will not secure freedom for all.

But it can be a lever, and Archimedes, in explaining the principles of the lever, was said to have declared to his friends: "Give me a place where I can stand, and I shall move the world."

My fellow inhabitants of this planet, let us take our stand here in this Assembly of nations. And let us see if we, in our own time, can move the world to a just and lasting peace.

Document XIV

President John F. Kennedy

TEST BAN TREATY

Remarks at the Signing-Treaty Room
of the White House*

October 7, 1963

In its first two decades, the Age of Nuclear Energy has been full of fear, yet never empty of hope. Today the fear is a little less and the hope a little greater. For the first time we have been able to reach an agreement which can limit the dangers of this age.

The agreement itself is limited, but its message of hope has been heard and understood not only by the peoples of the three originating nations but by the peoples and governments of the hundred other countries that have signed. This treaty is the first fruit of labors in which multitudes have shared—citizens, legislators, statesmen, diplomats and soldiers, too.

Soberly and unremittingly this nation, but never this nation alone, has sought the doorway to effective disarmament into a world where peace is secure. Today we have a beginning, and it is right for us to acknowledge all whose work across the years has helped make this beginning possible.

What the future will bring, no one of us can know. This first fruit of hope may or may not be followed by larger harvests. Even this limited treaty, great as it is with promise, can survive only if it has from others the determined support in letter and in spirit which I hereby pledge in behalf of the United States.

If this treaty fails, it will not be our doing, and even if it fails, we shall not regret that we have made this clear and honorable national

---

*Public Papers of the Presidents of the United States: John F. Kennedy. Containing the Messages Speeches and Statements of the President January 1 to November 22, 1963 (Washington, DC: US Government Printing Office, 1964), 765-66.

commitment to the cause of man's survival. For under this treaty we can and must still keep our vigil in defense of freedom.

But this treaty need not fail. This small step toward safety can be followed by others longer and less limited, if also harder in the taking. With our courage and understanding enlarged by this achievement, let us press onward in quest of man's essential desire for peace.

As President of the United States and with the advice and consent of the Senate, I now sign the instruments of ratification of this treaty.

Document XV

President John F. Kennedy

LET US EXHAUST EVERY AVENUE FOR PEACE*

Address at the University of Maine

October 19, 1963

One year ago this coming week, the United States and the world were gripped with a somber prospect of a military confrontation between the two great nuclear powers. The American people have good reason to recall with pride their conduct throughout that harrowing week. For they neither dissolved in panic nor rushed headlong into reckless belligerence. Well aware of the risks of resistance, they nevertheless refused to tolerate the Soviets' attempt to place nuclear weapons in this hemisphere, but recognized at the same time that our preparations for the use of force necessarily require a simultaneous search for fair and peaceful solutions.

A year ago it would have been easy to assume that all-out war was inevitable, that any agreement with the Soviets was impossible, and that an unlimited arms race was unavoidable. Today it is equally easy for some to assume that the Cold War is over, that all outstanding issues between the Soviets and our country can be quickly and satisfactorily settled, and that we shall now have, in the words of the Psalmist, an "abundance of peace so long as the moon endureth."

The fact of the matter is, of course, that neither view is correct. We have, it is true, made some progress on a long journey. We have achieved new opportunities which we cannot afford to waste. We have concluded with the Soviets a few limited, enforceable agreements or arrangements of mutual benefit to both sides and to the world.

But a change in the atmosphere and in emphasis is not a reversal of purpose. Mr. Khrushchev himself has said that there can be no coexistence in the field of ideology. In addition, there are still major areas

*Public Papers of the Presidents of the United States: John F. Kennedy. Containing the Messages, Speeches and Statements of the President .January 1 to November 22, 1963 (Washington, DC: US Government Printing Office, 1964), 795-97.

of tension and conflict, from Berlin to Cuba to Southeast Asia. The United States and the Soviet Union still have wholly different concepts of the world, its freedom, its future. We still have wholly different views on the so-called wars of liberation and the use of subversion. And so long as these basic differences continue, they cannot and should not be concealed. They set limits to the possibilities of agreements; and they will give rise to further crises, large and small, in the months and years ahead, both in the area of direct confrontation- Germany and the Caribbean-and in areas where events beyond our control could involve us both-areas such as Africa and Asia and the Middle East.

In times such as these, therefore, there is nothing inconsistent in signing an atmospheric nuclear test ban, on the one hand, and testing underground on the other; about being willing to sell to the Soviets our surplus wheat while refusing to sell strategic items; about probing their interest in a joint lunar landing while making a major effort to master this new environment; or about exploring the possibilities of disarmament while maintaining our stockpile of arms. For all of these moves, and all of these elements of American policy and Allied policy toward the Soviet Union, are directed at a single, comprehensive goal— namely, convincing the Soviet leaders that it is dangerous for them to engage in direct or indirect aggression, futile for them to attempt to impose their will and their system on other unwilling people, and beneficial to them, as well as to the world, to join in the achievement of a genuine and enforceable peace.

Historians report that in 1914, with most of the world already plunged in war, Prince Bulow, the former German Chancellor, said to the then Chancellor Bethmann-Hollweg, "How did it all happen?" And Bethmann-Hollweg replied, "Ah, if only one knew." My fellow Americans, if this planet is ever ravaged by nuclear war, if 300 million Americans, Russians and Europeans are wiped out by a sixty-minute nuclear exchange, if the pitiable survivors of that devastation can then endure the ensuing fire, poison, chaos and catastrophe, I do not want one of those survivors to ask another, "How did it all happen?" and to receive the incredible reply, "Ah, if only one knew."

Therefore, while maintaining our readiness for war, let us exhaust every avenue for peace. Let us always make clear our willingness to talk, if talk will help, and our readiness to fight, if fight we must. Let us resolve to be the masters, not the victims, of our history, controlling our own destiny without giving way to blind suspicion and emotion.

Document XVI

President John F. Kennedy

U.S. PARTICIPATION IN THE UNITED NATIONS

17th Annual Report to the Congress of the United States*

November 20, 1963

Pursuant to the provisions of the United Nations Participation Act, I transmit herewith the seventeenth Annual Report covering United States participation in the United Nations during 1962.

This record tells the story of deep United Nations engagement in the great issues of the 1960's. It demonstrates that despite the financial irresponsibility of some of its members, the Organization has, through executive action and parliamentary diplomacy, played an indispensable role in dealing with an impressive number of the world's problems.

The United Nations political relevance—and its developing capacity for effective action—is indicated by a brief look at several major aspects of world affairs and at what the United Nations did about them in 1962.

GREAT POWER CONFRONTATION

When the Soviet Union sought to alter the balance of nuclear power by installing missile bases in Cuba, the United Nations—as well as the Organization of American States—proved an important instrument in resolving the most dangerous crisis of the nuclear era. The Security Council served as a forum in which the United States Government made clear to the world that its actions, taken in concert with its neighbors of the Hemisphere, were the reasonable response of rational men to a sudden and unacceptable threat in their midst. The Secretary General, only recently elected to his post after a period as Acting Secretary General, provided a useful point of contact in the early stages of negotiations with the Soviet Union. The United Nations also could have

---

*Reprinted from *The Public Papers of the Presidents of the United States: John F. Kennedy. Containing the Messages, Speeches and Statements of the President. January 1 to November 22, 1963* (Washington, DC: US Government Printing Office, 1964), 880-82.

provided an on-site inspection service at short notice had the Cuban Government not refused to cooperate with the world organization, and made necessary a continuation of other means of surveillance in the interest of hemispheric security. Finally, the United Nations provided an appropriate place for negotiating the remaining issues after Soviet missiles had been withdrawn.

It was in 1962 that a major United Nations peacekeeping force in the Congo established a level of internal security which permitted a very substantial reduction in the size of that force. The Central Government of the Congo, assisted by the United Nations, has preserved (in the words of the Charter) its "territorial integrity and political independence—and thereby forestalled a threat to international peace—in the face of three attempts at secession: a communist-sponsored effort in the north, a local eruption in the interior, and a secession backed by outside interests in the south. Assisted by technical aid from most of the Specialized Agencies of the United Nations, the Government of the Congo has meanwhile increased its capacity to manage an economy of rich potential in the face of severe difficulties, including a crippling lack of trained manpower and experienced administrators.

In two other fields the United Nations has continued to be a vital instrument to effect a disengagement in important sectors of the great power confrontation. The Organization has served as a forum for encouraging an agreement for the cessation of nuclear weapon testing and for promoting progress toward general disarmament. It has served, as well, as a mechanism for negotiating legal principles and technical cooperation in outer space. We must be no less concerned with these persistent efforts to shape the future within the framework of the United Nations Charter than we are with United Nations operations designed to respond to the alarm bells of the present.

OTHER INTERNATIONAL PROBLEMS

During 1962 an impending conflict was averted in West New Guinea - the first territory administered by an international organization by the patient work of a United Nations mediator. In the Middle East the United Nations Emergency Force, the United Nations Truce Supervision Organization in Palestine, and the United Nations Relief and Works Agency for Palestine Refugees were on the job of removing and reducing tensions, and controlling those that could not yet be removed. In Kashmir, United Nations contingents patrolled under provisions of truce and cease- fire agreements. In Korea, a United Nations Commission stood ready to help in the unification of the country in accordance with resolutions of the General Assembly. (Since the end of 1962, the United Nations has begun another work of peacemaking, through an agreement for the disengagement in Yemen of the United Arab Republic and Saudi Arabia.)

FINANCING PEACEKEEPING

At the 17th General Assembly the United Nations received and then accepted the Advisory Opinion of the International Court of Justice that peacekeeping expenses of the United Nations in the Congo and the Middle East, earlier approved by the Assembly, are expenses of the Organization within the meaning of Article 17 of the Charter. The failure of member states to pay their related assessments would thus subject them to the loss-of-vote provisions of Article 19. The Court's opinion and its acceptance set the stage for what, based on later actions by the General Assembly, promises to produce a sturdier sense of financial responsibility on the part of most of the members.

COLONIAL QUESTIONS

Despite predictions of "another Congo," the United Nations trust territory of Ruanda-Urundi moved peacefully from dependence under Belgian administration to independence as the Republic of Rwanda and the Kingdom of Burundi and then to membership in the United Nations. The Organization continued to tackle the problems of nonviolent transition as awakening peoples moved steadily toward independence from old colonial patterns. The remnants of the world's colonial past still present some hard cases—the last precisely because they are the hardest—which will test the capacity of the world community, and of the United Nations, to devise the procedures and institutions of peaceful change.

It should come to us as no surprise that the struggle for national self-determination should be so closely linked with other fundamental questions of human rights. It has been so in our own country. As the decolonization process nears an end—with miraculously little bloodshed—men and nations can shift their attention from national freedom to the larger issue of individual freedom.

THE DRIVE FOR MODERNIZATION

Through its Specialized Agencies and regional commissions-its technical assistance and pre-investment work ... its civil role in the Congo ... its new projects such as the World Food Program, the World Weather Watch, and regional planning institutes ... its standard-setting and rule-making roles in such fields as maritime safety and international radio frequency allocations ... its useful reports and its many conferences—the United Nations moved ahead as the principal international executive agency of the Decade of Development. We continue to believe it possible, through vigorous international cooperation, to achieve an average annual rate of economic growth of five percent in the newly developing nations by the end of this decade.

In short, the United Nations in 1962 was confronted—in practical and operational ways—with a broad agenda of the great issues of our time. Like most institutions devised by man, the United Nations exhibited both accomplishments and short-comings. But despite noncooperation from some members and wavering support from others, the Organization moved significantly toward the goal of a peace system worldwide in scope. The United States will continue to lend vigorous support to the building of that system.

Document XVII

UNIVERSAL DECLARATION OF HUMAN RIGHTS

Preamble

Whereas recognition of the inherent dignity and of the equal and inalienable rights of all members of the human family is the foundation of freedom, justice and peace in the world,

Whereas disregard and contempt for human rights have resulted in barbarous acts which have outraged the conscience of mankind, and the advent of a world in which human beings shall enjoy freedom of speech and belief and freedom from fear and want has been proclaimed as the highest aspiration of the common people,

Whereas it is essential, if man is not to be compelled to have recourse, as a last resort, to rebellion against tyranny and oppression, that human rights should be protected by the rule of law,

Whereas it is essential to promote the development of friendly relations between nations.

Whereas the peoples of the United Nations have in the Charter reaffirmed their faith in fundamental human rights, in the dignity and worth of the human person and in the equal rights of men and women and have determined to promote social progress and better standards of life in larger freedom,

Whereas Member States have pledged themselves to achieve, in co-operation with the United Nations, the promotion of Universal respect for and observance of human rights and fundamental freedoms, Whereas a common understanding of these rights and freedoms is of the greatest importance for the full realization of this pledge,

---

From *Universal Declaration of Human Rights* by the United Nations General Assembly, ©1948. United Nations.

Now, therefore,
The General Assembly
proclaims this

Universal Declaration of Human Rights as a common standard of achievement for all peoples and all nations, to the end that every individual and every organ of society, keeping this Declaration constantly in mind, shall strive by teaching and education to promote respect for these rights and freedoms and by progressive measures, national and international, to secure their universal and effective recognition and observance, both among the peoples of Member States themselves and among the peoples of territories under their jurisdiction.

Article 1
All human beings are born free and equal in dignity and rights. They are endowed with reason and conscience and should act towards one another in a spirit of brotherhood.

Article 2
Everyone is entitled to all the rights and freedoms set forth in this Declaration, without distinction of any kind, such as race, colour, sex, language, religion, political or other opinion, national or social origin, property, birth or other status. Furthermore, no distinction shall be made on the basis of the political, jurisdictional or international status of the country or territory to which a person belongs, whether it be independent, trust, non self governing or under any other limitation of sovereignty.

Article 3
Everyone has the right to life, liberty and security of person.

Article 4
No one shall be held in slavery or servitude; slavery and the slave trade shall be prohibited in all their forms.

Article 5
No one shall be subjected to torture or to cruel, inhuman or degrading treatment or punishment.

Article 6

Everyone has the right to recognition everywhere as a person before the law.

Article 7

All are equal before the law and are entitled without any discrimination to equal protection of the law. All are entitled to equal protection against any discrimination in violation of this Declaration and against any incitement to such discrimination.

Article 8

Everyone has the right to an effective remedy by the competent national tribunals for acts violating the fundamental rights granted him by the constitution or by law.

Article 9

No one shall be subjected to arbitrary arrest, detention or exile.

Article 10

Everyone is entitled in full equality to a fair and public hearing by an independent and impartial tribunal, in the determination of his rights and obligations and of any criminal charge against him.

Article 11

1. Everyone charged with a penal offence has the right to be presumed innocent until proved guilty according to law in a public trial at which he has had all the guarantees necessary for his defence.
2. No one shall be held guilty of any penal offence on account of any act or omission which did not constitute a penal offence, under national or international law, at the time when it was committed. Nor shall a heavier penalty be imposed than the one that was applicable at the time the penal offence was committed.

Article 12

No one shall be subjected to arbitrary interference with his privacy, family, home or correspondence, nor to attacks upon his honour and reputation. Everyone has the right to the protection of the law against such interference or attacks.

Article 13
1. Everyone has the right to freedom of movement and residence within the borders of each state.
2. Everyone has the right to leave any country, including his own, and to return to his country.

Article 14
1. Everyone has the right to seek and to enjoy in other countries asylum from persecution.
2. This right may not be invoked in the case of prosecutions genuinely arising from non-political crimes or from acts contrary to the purposes and principles of the United Nations.

Article 15
1. Everyone has the right to a nationality.
2. No one shall be arbitrarily deprived of his nationality nor denied the right to change his nationality.

Article 16
1. Men and women of full age, without any limitation due to race, nationality or religion, have the right to marry and to found a family. They are entitled to equal rights as to marriage, during marriage and at its dissolution.
2. Marriage shall be entered into only with the free and full consent of the intending spouses.
3. The family is the natural and fundamental group unit of society and is entitled to protection by society and the State.

Article 17
1. Everyone has the right to own property alone as well as in association with others.
2. No one shall be arbitrarily deprived of his property.

Article 18
Everyone has the right to freedom of thought, conscience and religion; this right includes freedom to change his religion or belief, and freedom, either alone or in community with others and in public or private, to manifest his religion or belief in teaching, practice, worship and observance.

Article 19

Everyone has the right to freedom of opinion and expression; this right includes freedom to hold opinions without interference and to seek, receive and impart information and ideas through any media and regardless of frontiers.

Article 20

1. Everyone has the right to freedom of peaceful assembly and association.
2. No one may be compelled to belong to an association.

Article 21

1. Everyone has the right to take part in the government of his country, directly or through freely chosen representatives.
2. Everyone has the right of equal access to public service in his country.
3. The will of the people shall be the basis of the authority of government; this will shall be expressed in periodic and genuine elections which shall be by universal and equal suffrage and shall be held by secret vote or by equivalent free voting procedures.

Article 22

Everyone, as a member of society, has the right to a social security and is entitled to realization, through national effort and international co-operation and in accordance with the organization and resources of each State, of the economic, social and cultural rights indispensable for his dignity and the free development of his personality.

Article 23

1. Everyone has the right to work, to free choice of employment, to just and favourable conditions of work and to protection against unemployment.
2. Everyone, without any discrimination, has the right to equal pay for equal work.
3. Everyone who works has the right to just and favourable remuneration ensuring for himself and his family an existence worthy of human dignity, and supplemented, if necessary, by other means of social protection.
4. Everyone has the right to form and to join trade unions for the protection of his interests.

Article 24
Everyone has the right to rest and leisure, including reasonable limitation of working hours and periodic holidays with pay.

Article 25
1. Everyone has the right to a standard of living adequate for the health and well-being of himself and of his family, including food, clothing, housing and medical care and necessary social services, and the right to security in the event of unemployment, sickness, disability, widowhood, old age or other lack of livelihood in circumstances beyond his control.
2. Motherhood and childhood are entitled to special care and assistance. All children, whether born in or out of wedlock, shall enjoy the same social protection.

Article 26
1. Everyone has the right to education. Education shall be free, at least in the elementary and fundamental stages. Elementary education shall be compulsory. Technical and professional education shall be made generally available and higher education shall be equally accessible to all on the basis of merit.
2. Education shall be directed to the full development of the human personality and to the strengthening of respect for human rights and fundamental freedoms. It shall promote understanding, tolerance and friendship among all nations, racial or religious groups, and shall further the activities of the United Nations for the maintenance of peace.
3. Parents have a prior right to choose the kind of education that shall be given to their children.

Article 27
1. Everyone has the right freely to participate in the cultural life of the community, to enjoy the arts and to share in scientific advancement and its benefits.
2. Everyone has the right to the protection of the moral and material interests resulting from any scientific, literary or artistic production of which he is the author.

Article 28
Everyone is entitled to a social and international order in which the rights and freedoms set forth in this Declaration can be fully realized.

Article 29

1. Everyone has duties to the community in which alone the free and full development of his personality is possible.
2. In the exercise of his rights and freedoms, everyone shall be subject only to such limitations as are determined by law solely for the purpose of securing due recognition and respect for the rights and freedoms of others and of meeting the just requirements of morality, public order and the general welfare in a democratic society.
3. These rights and freedoms may in no case be exercised contrary to the purposes and principles of the United Nations.

Article 30

Nothing in this Declaration may be interpreted as implying for any State, group or person any right to engage in any activity or to perform any act aimed at the destruction of any of the rights and freedoms set forth herein.